Studies on the Ch

The Reform and Development of China's Rural Economy

Chief Editors:
Gao Shangquan *and* Chi Fulin

FOREIGN LANGUAGES PRESS   BEIJING

First Edition 1997

The project is aided by
(Hainan) China Foundation for Reform and Development Research.

ISBN 7-119-00697-5

© Foreign Languages Press, Beijing, 1997
Published by Foreign Languages Press
24 Baiwanzhuang Road, Beijing 100037, China
Printed by Foreign Languages Printing House
19 Chegongzhuang Xilu, Beijing 100044, China
Distributed by China International Book Trading Corporation
35 Chegongzhuang Xilu, Beijing 100044, China
P.O. Box 399, Beijing, China
Printed in the People's Republic of China

Foreword

Along with the development of the socialist market economy and the new problems it poses, how to improve agriculture so that it keeps up with China's economic advance has become a salient issue. Agriculture is now the weakest part of the national economy. If this trend continues, then not only will a solid foundation be lacking to ensure rapid overall economic development, but there also will be sharp social conflicts that will seriously influence national economic development and social stability. At present, the most outstanding contradictions in the rural areas are as follows: the contradiction between the demand for and supply of agricultural products results in continual price rises and inflationary pressure; the slow income increase of the farmers will delay the scheduled realization of the goal of farmers attaining a moderately high standard of living; and the failure to improve farmers' purchasing power and expand the rural consumption market will restrict the development of industry and the economy as a whole. From the long-term point of view, agriculture in China is also bedevilled by difficulties such as population increase and constant demands for a higher standard of living and the quickening of the process of industrialization in the countryside. What is more, agriculture is severely hampered by factors such as the chronic shrinking of arable land and weak infrastructure. Thus, from an overall and strategic point of view, the deepening of the rural reform is an imperative task if China is to succeed in developing agriculture, improving the rural areas and giving farmers a well-off standard of living.

In March 1995 the International Seminar on China's Rural Economic Reform was held jointly by the China (Hainan) Institute for Reform and Development, the Chinese Society of Economic Restructuring and the United Nations Development Program. Over a hundred experts from home and abroad gathered in Haikou, capital of Hainan Province, and held wide-ranging and profound discussions on many important issues arising from the course of China's rural economic reform. These included the reform of price policy and the purchase and sale system of agricutural and sideline products, village orgainzation and property rights structure, the outflow of surplus rural labor, the transformation of government functions and overall rural development.

This book is based on research done by the China (Hainan) Institute of Reform and Development, and papers and materials related to the seminar, as well as views announced by experts in the field of agriculture. Valuable research and deliberations on China's rural reform made by many experts and the experience of rural development in other countries are both included in the book.

Gao Shangquan and Chi Fulin served as chief editors of this book. The latter was also responsible for finalizing the manuscripts. The chief compiler was Zhu Huayou.

Heartfelt thanks to the (Hainan) China Foundation for Reform and Development Research for financial aid for the publication of this book.

The authors
June 1995

Contents

Chapter I
Perfecting Macroeconomic Policies and Deepening Rural Economic Reform — 1
- I. China's Rural Economic Reform Is a Breakthrough for the National Reform — 1
- II. The Importance of the Rural Reform and Development to Macro Stability — 25
- III. China's Rural Problems and Agricultural Policies — 29

Chapter II
Rural Land System Reform — 48
- I. Problems in the Land-Use System — 48
- II. Land Circulation and Scale Management — 55
- III. Land Shares as a Form of Cooperative Economy — 76

Chapter III
The Marketization of the Purchase and Sales Systems of Agricultural Products — 83
- I. Pushing Forward the Reform of the Purchase and Sales Systems with Marketization as the Objective — 83
- II. Grain Policies and Supply and Demand — 101
- III. The Construction of the Market System and the Founding of the National Unified Market — 125

Chapter IV
Migration of Surplus Rural Labor and Urbanization of Rural Areas — 149
- I. Migration of Surplus Rural Labor During the Economic Restructuring — 149
- II. The Development of Township Enterprises — 168

III. The Construction of Small Towns　176

Chapter V
Changing the Functions of the Government and Coordinated Development in Rural Areas　181
   I. Government Functions and Measures of Macro Control　181
   II. The Development of Rural Industrialization　193
   III. Coordinated Development of Urban and Rural Areas　203

Chapter I
Perfecting Macroeconomic Policies and Deepening Rural Economic Reform

I. China's Rural Economic Reform Is a Breakthrough for the National Reform

(I) Carrying Out China's Rural Economic Reform by Stages

From the end of 1978, when the Third Plenary Session of the 11th National Congress of the Communist Party of China (CPC) was held, to 1994 China's agricultural reform went through the following three major stages: The first stage was from 1978 to 1984, when China set up and gradually implemented the contract responsibility system based on the household and with remuneration linked to output in the rural areas. The second stage was from 1985 to 1991, when China reformed the system of state monopoly purchase and quotas, and gradually lifted controls from the market and prices of agricultural products. The third stage was from 1992 to 1994, when the country started the transition to the rural market economy in an all-round way.

1. Setting up and extensively carrying out the contract responsibility system based on the household and with remuneration linked to output.

The agricultural reform started with the Third Plenary Session of the CPC's 11th National Congress, held in December 1978. The session paid particular attention to agricultural problems: "The session holds that the whole Party must concentrate its main energies on the development of agriculture, because agriculture as the foundation of the national economy has suffered serious damage in recent years and as a whole is very weak now.... For this purpose, we must first mobilize the socialist enthusiasm of China's hundreds of millions of peasants, must be fully concerned with their material interests economically and truly guarantee their democratic rights politically." In accordance with these ideological guidelines the plenary session put forward a series of political and economic measures for developing agricultural production. The adoption of these measures was aimed at lightening the burden on peasants, mobilizing their initiative and freeing them from anxiety.

China's rural economic reform started with the contract responsibility system based on the household and with remuneration linked to output, commonly known as the fixing of output quotas based on the household or the contract responsibility system based on the household.

At the start of the rural economic reform in the 1980s China's rural contract responsibility system based on the household confronted serious political, theoretical and ideological obstacles. At that time, there was no single Party or government document supporting the fixing of output quotas based on the household. On the contrary, some documents clearly expressed negative attitudes toward the measure. However, it needs to be specially stressed that, along with the nationwide discussion in 1979 of the question of practice being the only criterion to judge the truth, people began to bravely break the ideological shackles which had hampered their thinking for quite a long time. It was in this situation, characterized by the relaxing of political ideology, that the broad masses of peasants and cadres in the rural areas started to sum up their historical experiences and explore the road of rural reform, by fixing output quotas based on the household in particular, in accordance with local conditions.

Setting up and extensively carrying out the contract responsibility system based on the household and with remuneration linked to output, and the reform of—and eventual abolition of —the people's commune were two major features of the first stage of China's agricultural reform. These two reforms advanced virtually side by side.

CHAPTER I PERFECTING MACROECONOMIC POLICIES

In October 1976, when the "gang of four" was being smashed, China's economy, including the rural economy, was on the verge of collapse. The annual income per capita of one third of the country's agricultural production brigades was less than 40 RMB yuan (about 25 US dollars according the exchange rate at that time), and the grain ration per capita was less than 150 kg (nearly 200 kg in south China, where paddy rice is mainly grown). More than 200 million peasants did not have enough to eat and wear, relying on government-supplied relief grains. In this situation the main leaders of the CPC Central Committee continued to carry out the "left" line, and so the peasants' urgent requirements for changing the situation in which they had no incentive for production, private plots and rural markets were abolished and sideline production was forbidden went unheeded.

In 1978 Anhui Province suffered from the most serious drought in 100 years: Many reservoirs dried up; the province ran short of drinking water for both people and animals; the output of summer grains was reduced; autumn planting met with difficulties; the cultivated land was parched and cracked; and wheat and rape could not grow at all. After close investigation and study the leaders of the CPC's Anhui Provincial Committee, who had held full discussions with both cadres and the masses, called for all peasants in the province to try every means to grow half a *mu* (one *mu*=1/15 ha) of "life-saving wheat." They allowed individuals to develop farmland which it was impracticable for the collectives to till. In addition, commune members were encouraged to open up wasteland to grow wheat, on which the government would not impose any levy or compulsory purchase. It meant the adoption of an unusual method—"tiding over the drought by borrowing land."

Although the fixing of output quotas based on the household was carried out in some regions, serious differences of opinion on this question existed within the central government and among local cadres at various levels. The essence of the dispute was whether the fixing of output quotas based on the household meant adhering to the socialist road or to the capitalist road. The new system nearly foundered in some places because of such

3

ideological disputes. But in the end the remarkable results achieved through fixing output quotas based on the household gradually convinced everyone of its practicality, thus forming a more favorable social environment of public opinion for its universal adoption.

From September 14 to 22, 1980, the CPC Central Committee held a special symposium attended by the first secretaries of the CPC Party committees of all provinces, autonomous regions and centrally administered municipalities to discuss how to perfect the agricultural production responsibility system. A summary of the symposium was promulgated, expounding for the first time in the form of a formal document of the Central Committee the nature of the fixing of the output quotas based on the household, and clearly pointed out: "On the condition of socialist industry, socialist commerce and collective agriculture occupying absolute predominance, and under the leadership of production brigades, the practice of the fixing of output quotas based on the household is part and parcel of the socialist economy and does not mean straying from the socialist track. So people don't need to worry about the danger of the restoration of capitalism." This document was warmly received by the peasants, thus quickening the development of the fixing of output quotas based on the household.

The preliminary achievements some regions made through the practice of this new system prompted many other places to adopt the method. In spite of serious natural disasters in 1980 the agricultural production of Anhui, Gansu, Guizhou and Shandong provinces and the Inner Mongolia Autonomous Region, which had all adopted the fixing of output quotas based on the household, increased by a large margin, a fact which greatly encouraged the cadres and masses of other provinces to make up their minds to follow suit. From then on, the fixing of output quotas based on the household was not only carried out in remote mountain areas, but plains and coastal regions, and in both poor and rich production brigades. The result was that all these places without exception increased their agricultural production.

The CPC 12th National Congress held in September 1982 reaffirmed the fixing of the output quotas based on the house-

CHAPTER I PERFECTING MACROECONOMIC POLICIES

hold. Hu Yaobang pointed out in his report, Initiating a New Situation of Socialist Modernization in an All-Round Way: "In recent years, various forms of production responsibility systems have further emancipated the productive forces and must be pursued for quite a long time to come. We can only gradually perfect them on the basis of practical experience and must not make changes rashly against the will of the people. Nor must we take the road back." In November 1982 the CPC Central Committee held the Rural Ideological and Political Work Meeting and the Meeting of Agricultural Secretaries, at which the document titled Certain Questions on Current Rural Economic Policies was formulated. It was printed and distributed on January 2, 1983. This document fully affirmed and spoke highly of the fixing of output quotas based on the household, and pointed out: "Since the Third Plenary Session of the CPC's 11th National Congress, tremendous changes have taken place in China's rural areas. The change with the most profound influence is the universal practice of various forms of agricultural production systems, in which the contract responsibility system based on the household and with remuneration linked to output is playing the leading role. This system follows the principle of linking unified and disparate operations, thus bringing into full play the collectives' advantages and individual enthusiasm. Following the promulgation of the document, 1983 became a year when China's rural reform developed in depth, and the fixing of output quotas based on the household rapidly became a main economic form in the countryside. By the end of 1983 some 179 million rural households had adopted the fixing of output quotas based on the household, making up 94.5 percent of the country's total.

During the course of the rural reform the leading bodies of the people's communes and production brigades in some regions had fallen into a state of paralysis or semi-paralysis, and much work had no one in charge of it. So they were not able to undertake the heavy economic and political tasks. The resolution of the CPC Central Committee—Certain Questions on Current Rural Economic Policies—issued on January 2, 1983 put forward for the first time the reform of the system of the people's communes and pointed out that the reform would be carried out from two aspects, i.e., the practice of the production responsibility system, especially the contract responsibility system based on the household and with remuneration linked to output, and the implementation of the separation of government administration from commune management.

As a matter of fact, the practice of the contract responsibility system based on the household and with remuneration linked to output has done away with the highly centralized management system of the communes and the attitude of "all eating from the same big pot," which stifled initiative in the past. As to the separation of government administration from commune management, the CPC Central Committee adopted extremely careful and steady reform principles, pointing out that "the system of integrating government administration with commune management should be replaced by the separation of government administration from commune management step by step. The replacement will not be carried out unless the people's communes are ready for the change. Before the separation of government administration from commune management, communes and brigades should perform their administrative functions to ensure the normal operation of political work. After the separation of government administration from commune management, organizations of political power at the basic levels should be set up in accordance with the Constitution." Under the unified leadership of the CPC Central Committee, Sichuan, Anhui, Jilin, Henan and Gansu, which took the lead in practicing the fixing of output quotas based on the household, made experiments in separating government administration from commune management so as to accumulate experience.

On October 12, 1983 the CPC Central Committee and the State Council formally promulgated the Circular on Separating Government Administration from Commune Management and Setting Up Township Governments. The circular pointed out: "Along with the reform of the rural economic system, the existing rural system which involves integrating government administration with commune management is not appropriate. The Consti-

CHAPTER I PERFECTING MACROECONOMIC POLICIES

tution clearly specifies that township governments should be set up in the countryside and government administration must be separated from commune management. Separating government administration from commune management and setting up township governments should be connected with the election of deputies to township people's congresses and should, in general, be finished before the end of 1984."

The change in the people's commune system went on smoothly. By the spring of 1985 the work in China's rural areas on separating government administration from commune management and setting up township governments had been completed. Before the founding of townships China had over 56,000 communes; after the separation of government administration from commune management, 91,138 township (town) people's governments were set up, under which were over 940,000 village committees. The completion of separating government administration from commune management and setting up township governments marked the formal end of the people's commune system in the rural areas throughout the country.

2. The initiation of the reform of the circulation system of agricultural products marked the expansion of the agricultural reform from the micro to the macro dimension.

The extensive practice of the contract responsibility system based on the household and with remuneration linked to output in China's rural areas emancipated China's peasants in two aspects: 1. property rights; and 2. status. Though these aspects were incomplete at first, the preliminary conditions started to emerge for the overall development of the rural commodity economy in China.

During the course of the rural reform the peasants have gradually won more freedom to engage in economic activities, while obtaining more property rights. It is the basic guiding principle of the rural reform to show full concern for the peasants' material interests economically and guarantee their democratic rights. Since 1978 the CPC Central Committee and the State Council have worked out and issued a series of important policies and some documents which have helped to eliminate some of the fetters of the old system, such as by changing the principle of taking food grains as the key link, allowing peasants to engage in household sideline occupations and develop a diversified economy, allowing various commercial organizations and individuals in the countryside to engage in transportation and sales activities, and allowing peasants to engage in various trades under the premise of supplying a sufficient quantity of food grains by themselves. All these are directional changes in the long-standing policies on restricting peasants' freedom of operation and personal freedom. Between 1979 and 1985, 45.772 million rural laborers transferred to non-agricultural fields. In addition, several hundred thousand to one million rural people moved to cities to engage in commercial and service activities. The number of peasants who leave their homes to serve as temporary workers totals six million every year, and each year cities and towns employ about one million peasants on average. In short, by 1985, thanks to the stimulation of the rural reform, nearly one fifth of rural laborers had changed their jobs, homes or actual social status. Thus essential changes had taken place in the peasants' modes of life, production and social contacts. This shows that the peasants, who make up 80 percent of the total population in China enjoy the freedom of changing their occupations and social status in step with economic development.

In the course of the fixing of output quotas based on the household, the CPC Central Committee and State Council began to lift the long-standing strict ban on allowing peasants to enter the circulation field. In 1984 the central government showed great concern for the development of rural commodity economy. On January 1, 1984 the CPC Central Committee promulgated the Circular on Rural Work, which pointed out once again: "Only as long as we continue to develop commodity production can we further promote the social division of labor, push the productive forces to a new level, make the rural areas rich and prosperous, enable our cadres to learn how to make use of the relations between commodities and money and the law of value to serve the planned economy and speed up China's socialist agricultural modernization."

CHAPTER I PERFECTING MACROECONOMIC POLICIES

In accordance with the aforementioned decision of the central government, the State Commission for Restructuring the Economy, the Ministry of Commerce and the Ministry of Agriculture, Animal Husbandry and Fisheries decided to adopt the following reform measures in the field of circulation of agricultural products: First, as for developing multichannel circulation, they pointed out that "China should develop a diversified economy, including state-owned, collectively-owned and individual economies, adopt various economic forms and implement multichannel circulation. Farmers should be encouraged to enter the circulation field, and should be allowed to engage in the exchange of commodities. We should not restrict farmers' business activities and allow them to become an important supplementary force to the state-owned commerce and supply and marketing cooperatives, depending on actual conditions."

Second, with regard to the readjustment of the policies on purchasing and marketing agricultural and sideline products, they decided to go on reducing the varieties for planned purchase and purchase by state quotas. The three varieties for planned purchase are grain (rice, wheat and corn), oil-bearing crops (peanuts, vegetable seeds and cotton seeds), and cotton (cotton within the grades and cotton linters). Eighteen varieties for purchase by state quotas will be reduced to nine varieties, i.e., pigs, jute and bluish dogbane, ramie, tea, cattle hides (only the hides of cattle slaughtered by the state), sheep's wool, bamboo, *gaozhu* (a kind of bamboo) and vegetables (only those destined for large and medium-sized cities and the main industrial and mining areas). The government will lift control from the purchase and marketing of goat and sheep skins, cashmere, beef, mutton, fresh eggs, apples, oranges and tangerines, and tung oil. Flexible policies on the management of Chinese herbal medicines and forestry products will be adopted. Chinese herbal medicines purchased in accordance with state quotas will be reduced from 30 varieties to 24. Control of small amounts of timber and timber products, as well as bamboo among forestry products will be completely relaxed, and various channels will be made available for their handling. Meanwhile, some timber markets will be opened and farmers will be organized to regulate timber resources.

Third, as to improving the methods of managing prices, it was specified that "all agricultural and sideline products which are purchased according to the state's plan or quotas and included in the plan will be purchased at the planned purchase prices. Products superfluous to the planned purchase and purchase by the state quotas, and non-planned products will be purchased and marketed after negotiations, and the purchase prices will rise or fall according to market supply and demand."

Fourth, as to the reform of the wholesale system of agricultural and sideline products, it was required "to change the wholesale system featured by unified purchase and supply according to administrative divisions and levels, and unreasonable operational links should be abolished. The basic operational links of agricultural and sideline products are in counties, where special wholesale companies may be set up."

Fifth, as to quickening the reform of the supply and marketing cooperative system, it was required that the supply and marketing cooperatives make a breakthrough in helping farmers to become shareholders, expand the scope of operations and services, and manage distribution according to work, prices, etc., on the principle of changing the "government-run" into the "nongovernment-run."

Sixth, as for actively developing the processing industry of agricultural and sideline products, "this will help to satisfy the needs of improving the people's livelihood, perfect China's food structure, make agricultural and sideline products more beneficial and help solve peasants' difficulties in purchasing and selling products. So we should spare no effort to do the work well." And, "The government should adopt favorable policies to support the development of the processing industry in rural areas."

Seventh, as to greatly developing communications and transportation and the facilities for commodity operation, it was stressed that "due to the constant development of the production and circulation of rural commodities, and the steady expansion of horizontal economic connections, the stumbling blocks of

CHAPTER I PERFECTING MACROECONOMIC POLICIES

inadequate communications, transportation and commercial facilities are becoming more prominent. From now on, we should mobilize all forces to actively develop rural communications and transportation, and speed up the building of commodity facilities. While planning the production of commodities, each locality should plan the relevant processing, storage and transportation. It is imperative to handle the circulation of rural commodities well."

On January 1, 1985 the CPC Central Committee and the State Council promulgated the Ten Policies on Further Enlivening the Rural Economy, which declared, "From this year, except for one or two varieties, the government will no longer issue unified and fixed state purchase quotas for agricultural products. Purchase by contract or through the market will be adopted, depending on local circumstances." And "The unified state purchase of grain and cotton will be abolished and will be replaced by purchase by contract. Ahead of the sowing season the commercial departments will consult with farmers before signing purchasing contracts. As for the purchase of grain by contract, the government has decided that 30 percent of the harvested grain will be paid for at the original unified state purchase price, and the remaining 70 percent will be paid for at the price for above-quota grain. The grain not included in the purchase contract can be sold on the market. If the grain prices on the market are lower than the original unified state purchase prices, the state will purchase an unlimited amount of grain to protect farmers' interests. As for the purchase of cotton, 30 percent will be paid for at the original unified state purchase price and the rest at the price for above-quota cotton in north China; in south China 40 percent will be paid for at the original unified state purchase price, and 60 percent will be regarded as above-quota cotton. The remains may be sold by peasants independently. <u>The fixed state purchase of pigs, aquatic products and vegetables for large and medium-sized cities and industrial and mining areas will be gradually abolished and farmers will be allowed to sell them on the market freely</u> and at prices fluctuating along with market changes and according to quality. As to when the flexible policies will be adopted and how to implement them step by step, each locality will decide by itself. After the adoption of the measures, the state-owned commercial sector should actively operate and participate in the market regulation. Meanwhile, feasible measures must be taken to guarantee the interests of urban consumers. After abolishing the unified and fixed state purchase, agricultural products are no longer restricted by the original division of operation and can be circulated through various channels. The units engaged in selling, processing and consuming agricultural products may directly sign purchase contracts with farmers, who may sign sales contracts with the units concerned on their own initiative through cooperative organizations or set up their own producers' associations." In addition, "no unit should issue mandatory production plans to farmers."

However, as compared with the first stage of the rural reform, the reform of the circulation system of agricultural products involves more aspects of interests and is more complicated. The essence of the second stage of the reform is a profound readjustment of the relations between the state and farmers, and will inevitably lead to new changes in the relations between urban and rural areas, workers and peasants and in the interest relations among the various sectors of the national economy. The aim of the unified and fixed state purchase was to redistribute the national income in the name of purchasing and selling commodities. Each portion of agricultural products sold by farmers to the state meant a contribution to the state; each agricultural product purchased by workers, staff or enterprises was equivalent to obtaining welfare from the state. Hence, the reform of the unified and fixed state purchase system, which focuses on exchanges at equal value, will unavoidably affect the readjustment of the basic interests of all urban and rural producers, consumers and operators, and will surely lead to profound changes of the overall economic setup and organizational forms.

3. Approaching the market economy in an all-round way.

In the 1980s China scored tremendous successes in the agricultural reform as a whole, in spite of certain problems. First of all, agricultural production increased by a large margin, and the

CHAPTER I PERFECTING MACROECONOMIC POLICIES

land output rate and the production rate of agricultural laborers improved. At the same time, the focus on grain as the "key link" was changed and the agricultural production structure was gradually optimized. Meanwhile, township enterprises, which suddenly came to the fore, have played an important role in developing the rural economy, and farmers' incomes have increased by a large margin and their livelihoods have improved remarkably.

Some experts have divided the reform of the rural economy into the following three stages:

The first stage, or the breakthrough stage (1978-1984): During this period the rural reform progressed smoothly. The contract responsibility system based on the household and with remuneration linked to output, which started in certain pioneer regions and later spread all over the country, was regarded as an expedient measure to provide peasants with enough food and clothing at the beginning, but a few years later was affirmed as the long- or medium-term basic economic operation system in rural areas.

The second stage, or all-round exploratory stage (1985-1988): After 1985 the Chinese government worked out some important measures to further reform the unified and fixed state purchase of agricultural products and change the rural production structure. The unified state purchase of grain was changed into purchase by contract and through the market, i.e., a "double-track system." Except for four kinds of products such as cotton, controls were lifted from the prices of other agricultural products, and the prices were then determined by supply and demand. Farmers were encouraged to run various forms of township and village enterprises and develop different types of nonagricultural production.

The third, or readjusting and deepening stage (from the autumn of 1988 to the present): In August 1988 the Chinese government put forward the principle of improving and rectifying economic work so as to restrain inflation, readjust the industrial structure and rectify the situation in which economic results had plummeted sharply. During the three-year improvement and readjustment period, due to a shortage of capital, the sluggish market and some administrative interference, the readjustment of the rural production structure, especially the development of township enterprises, was hampered, and the income of farmers fluctuated for the first time since the initiation of the reform. However, rural reform still made great progress in spite of the fact that some of the reform measures were carelessly worked out. The first was the reform of the grain purchase and marketing system. In April 1991, on the basis of the localities carrying out grain reform on their own initiative, China raised the grain sales prices in a unified way. They were increased again in the following year, by 140 percent. Consequently, the purchasing prices were almost equivalent to the sales prices. Under this financial pressure, the pace of grain reform greatly exceeded the speed that people had expected. The second was the growth of the market for agricultural products. In October 1990 the central government set up a wholesale wheat market in Zhengzhou, and nine regional wholesale markets and a number of standardized rural fairs developed rapidly throughout the country, thus creating material bases and channels for finally abolishing the planned allocation of major agricultural products.

(II) Adhering to Market Orientation Is the Quintessence of the Rural Economic Reform of China

1. The household contract system is the micro-economic system's foundation for the growth of the market system.

The achievements of China's rural reform are especially manifested in the setting up of the household contract system, the growth of the market system and the emergence of township enterprises. Among these there exist logical relations. Without the household contract system there would be neither the growth of the market nor the emergence of township enterprises.

The fact that the household contract system has become the core of the basic achievements of the rural reform in China has profound theoretical connotations. People often say that the vitality of this system originated in the separation of ownership from operational rights, i.e., the farmers have autonomy over their operations on publicly owned land. However, an overall

CHAPTER I PERFECTING MACROECONOMIC POLICIES

survey of the economic essence of this system reveals that the changes in the rural economic and social relations resulting from this system have gone far beyond the simple separation of ownership from operation right. First of all, the household contract system has led to profound changes in rural property relations. During the period of the people's communes rural properties belonged, both theoretically and legally to the farmers organized in collectives. However, such ownership was in name only. After the founding of the household contract system, changes took place in the existing form of original collectively owned properties, i.e., though the farmers do not have ownership, they have occupation and use rights. On the other hand, they also have independent property ownership, including the right to make investment in the land and obtain added income therefrom. Farmers, no matter whether they are engaged in the contract economy or self-operated economy, enjoy complete ownership after they have paid taxes and handed in other necessary fees to the state. Farmers' property rights have thus been re-established, greatly spurring their enthusiasm for production. Second, their status is one of considerable freedom nowadays. The people's communes adopted the system of management of paramilitary organizations, and farmers were restricted in their work and movements. But since the founding of the household contract system they have not only obtained freedom for economic activities within the contracted fields, but also the freedom of economic activities in the self-operated economic fields. They may not only engage in operational activities in agricultural production, they also may leave the land or even the country.

The market economy regulates economic life mainly with the market as guidance. The market is the total sum of exchange relations. Exchanges are carried out by the market's main bodies, or economic entities. Not all economic units may become the main bodies of the market. The basic characteristics of the market's main bodies are distinct ownership relations and independent operation rights. The first and foremost contribution that the household contract system has made to the development of the market system is that the system has created a large number of market main bodies, thus enabling millions of peasants and rural households to enter the market. Peasants have been turned into commodity producers and operators with independent property and operation rights from being merely laborers. Peasants have started to organize and readjust their production and operation activities with the market as the center. The disposition of rural resources is being allocated more and more by the market. Hence the household contract system has laid a micro organizational foundation for the market economy system in the rural areas. On this foundation, <u>peasants' self-service organizations, rural associated economic entities, rural privately owned enterprises, rural collectively owned enterprises and various other market main bodies have sprung up and have grown rapidly</u>, thus forming a multi-level, multi-form market system with diversified economic elements and creating a prosperous rural commodity economy. Of course, this does not mean that the market system only needs the household contract system. The founding of the market economy system should also include market standardization and the setting up of market order as well as the government's effective macro control. However, there is no doubt that the household contract system has made tremendous contributions to the setting up of the rural market economy, which no other reform measures can match.

The appearance of the market main bodies has powerfully pushed forward the development of the relations between rural commodities and currency. Thanks to the widespread adoption of the household contract system throughout the country, and the great increase in the prices of agricultural products, the labor and production rates in agriculture have been raised markedly, and the output of agricultural products has increased by a large margin. The increase in agricultural production has alleviated the long-lasting shortage of agricultural products and has provided material conditions for the state to change the original planned and centrally controlled production, purchase and marketing of such products. On this basis, the state has adopted a series of measures: First of all, China replaced unified state purchase of grain, cotton and edible oil by contract purchase, lifted controls

CHAPTER I PERFECTING MACROECONOMIC POLICIES

from the purchase and marketing prices of the overwhelming majority of agricultural products, allowed peasants to sell products not included in the purchase contract as they wish, and encouraged free competition through various channels. Now, of the total sales volume of agricultural and side-line products sold by peasants, that purchased according to contracts makes up less than one fourth; market regulation in the circulation of agricultural and sideline products occupies the dominant position.

At the start of the rural reform China neither took township enterprises as one of the objectives of rural development, nor expected that township enterprises would become the main pillar of the rural economy over a decade or so. Indeed it is a surprising achievement. However, township enterprises are truly an inevitable outcome of the rural reform, which is rooted in the quick growth of the relations between rural commodities and currency circulation in the course of reform as well as in the rapid growth of the rural market system. After the setting up of the household contract system rural productivity was raised and farmers, with a certain amount of surplus capital, had the ability to make preliminary accumulation and investment. Meanwhile, a great number of laborers freed from work on the land needed new jobs. In addition, the government readjusted its policies, allowing farmers to engage in the circulation and processing of agricultural and sideline products, and other nonagricultural production. These conditions allowed key elements of agriculture to engage in new areas of production. Under these circumstances, farmers in areas with a large labor force but little land, and autonomy over the disposition of resources, were able to engage in other economic activities. Different from the household contract system, this trend necessitated the seeking out of and satisfying market demand.

Township enterprises encapsulate the new market economic system of rural reform and development. First, as the outcome of the market environment, township enterprises have strong congenital ability to adapt to the changes in the market, exist beyond the state's direct planning, conduct all their economic activities in the market, decide their output according to sales, have strong ability to sell their products, take operation risks by themselves and handle operations on their own. Township enterprises have flexible market employment mechanisms and are highly adaptable to changes in production demand. With market orientation as the center, township enterprises can basically meet the demands of the key elements of enterprise organizations in the market economy. Therefore, as compared with state-owned enterprises in the planned economy, their economic mechanisms have more vitality and better ability to adapt to the transition from the planned economy system to the market economy system. Second, during their growth period township enterprises have promoted the transition of not just the rural economy but also the national economy in a market-oriented direction. Third, township enterprises have powerfully verified the proposition that a socialist country can also pursue a market economy, and this can be more efficient than a planned economy.

2. The second-step reform in the countryside with the reduction of direct planned control as the focus has further accelerated the growth of the market system.

Though the contract responsibility system based on the household and with remuneration linked to output has created the micro-organizational bases for the development of the rural market economy, such bases have many shortcomings as compared with the market main bodies in the sense of the actual commodity economy, due to the influence of small-scale peasant economy and the trammels of the "double-track system" of the planned and market economic systems existing side by side.

(1) Non-commodity economic activities occupy quite a large percentage. The current productive forces in the countryside determine that farmers do not seek the highest returns for the least investment in complete accordance with the law of value before they have enough to eat, fulfill the tasks of the unified and fixed state purchase, and withhold retained funds. This phase is the turning point between peasant commodity economic activity and non-commodity economic activity. At this critical point farmers' economic actions can not be controlled by themselves. Only economic activity beyond the critical point is true commod-

ity economic behavior.

(2) The ownership relations are not clear. The land and collectively owned enterprises in the countryside now belong to the collectives in name, but actually no one owns them as no one has the right to put them on the market as commodities. Only when such ownership relations become clear can the market's accelerating role be brought into play, can ownership flow according to economic laws and can the market play its due role in effectively disposing of resources.

(3) Incomplete functioning of products. For a long period of time the government had made agriculture continually provide construction capital to the state in an invisible form (i.e. price distribution) and forcefully deprived peasants of their power to manipulate some products and fix their prices by practising fixed purchase and fixed prices so as to guarantee the stability of the quantity of agricultural products needed by the state. In 1991 the grain purchased by the state according to contracts came to about 60 billion kg; over 95 percent of cotton was solely controlled by supply and marketing cooperatives; and tobacco and silkworm cocoons were monopolized by special units.

After the first step was taken in the rural reform (the adoption of the contract responsibility system based on the household with remuneration linked to output), the second step weakened the control by direct planning step by step, reduced administrative interference and constantly strengthened the growth of market mechanisms. Thus farmers were encouraged to decide their own economic activities according to market rules. Consequently, the rural economic market economy has developed vigorously. This is mainly manifested in the following aspects:

(1) The scope of the rural economy regulated by the market has constantly been enlarged. In 1978, 113 kinds of agricultural products were directly under the state's control. Now, except for a small number of agricultural and sideline products vital to the national economy and the people's livelihood, such as grain, cotton, tobacco and silkworm cocoons, state control over agricultural and sideline products has been completely lifted. Of the total volume of agricultural and sideline products sold by farm-

ers, those purchased according to state plans make up less than one fourth. This indicates that in the circulation of agricultural and sideline products market regulation plays the leading role.

(2) A rural market system is being formed. Since 1979 the number of China's rural markets has doubled; the business volume has increased by 15 times; the average market scale has grown sevenfold; and wholesale markets and various specialized markets for agricultural and sideline products have been set up and expanded to over 1,600, or a more than fourfold increase over the 1983 figure. In addition, markets where industrial products are traded and markets for means of production, labor, capital, technology and information have sprung up rapidly.

(3) More farmers have entered the market and circulation fields. Now they are not only producers of agricultural and sideline products, but also important forces to enliven commodity circulation and boost the market. According to official statistics, China now has 6.392 million nongovernmental purchasing and marketing organizations in the countryside, with 13.988 million employees. Township enterprises alone have 5.1 million people engaged in purchasing raw and processed materials and selling the products. Of the total retail sales volume of agricultural and sideline products, that of farmers' commercial organizations makes up one third. Moreover, the figure is increasing rapidly.

(4) A new commodity circulation order is being formed. The rural markets not only bring about tangible benefits, they also bring about intangible benefits though their influence on prices and their roles in opening businesses, collection and distribution, information exchange, balancing supply and demand, improving business efficiency and cutting circulation costs. They have made circulation links tighter, doing away with the traditional, isolated and multi-level planned circulation system.

3. Township enterprises epitomize the market nature of the rural reform.

The workers and staff of township enterprises are ex-farmers, and their living quarters are thousands of rural households. As compared with state-owned enterprises in the old planned econo-

CHAPTER I PERFECTING MACROECONOMIC POLICIES

my system, such enterprises have obvious advantages: a. At present they do not basically need facilities for living quarters, so township enterprises are not directly burdened with running social service undertakings. b. As the rural areas have surplus labor, the cost of labor in the countryside is quite low. c. As farmers run enterprises by themselves the direct relations between farmers and enterprises are favorable to the handling of the contradictions between industry and agriculture. d. Since there is no "iron rice bowl" in the countryside any more, township enterprises have no heavy burden of paying retirement pensions, and of providing jobs for employees' children. Thanks to these characteristics and advantages, township enterprises are more able to adapt to the transition from the planned economy to the market economy.

The great progress made by China's township enterprises has made at least three important contributions to the founding of the socialist market economic system: a. During their development, township enterprises struck powerful blows at the old highly-centralized and unified planned economic system, thus pushing forward the transition of the rural economy and that of the nation as a whole in the direction of a market economy. b. They have clearly verified that a socialist country can pursue a market economy, and that the market economy can work better and more efficiently than the planned economy in a socialist country. c. Township enterprises have provided rich practical experience for deepening the reform and setting up a socialist market economic system.

4. The leading social and economic causes of the growth of the rural market system.

It is unquestionable that the rural reform is playing a leading role in China's economic reform as a whole. There are many manifestations of this, and, in a word, it is the growth leader of the new market economy system. This is by no means an accidental case, but has profound social and economic causes. First, the peasants, who suffered the most under the old system, voice the strongest demands for reforming it. The old planned economic system sacrificed peasants' interests in many aspects. The unified and fixed state purchase was actually a means of distributing the national income, which concealed serious exploitation of peasants economically. The people's communes adopted compulsory means beyond economic ones to control the people in the countryside, thus strengthening such exploitation organizationally and politically. The peasants nursed grievances against this system for quite a long time. Therefore once political pressure was lifted and the government realized the necessity of carrying out the reform, these grievances tended to burst out immediately, thus opening the road for China's reform. Second, the economic relations in the countryside are fairly simple. The socialization of agricultural production is low, the division of labor is underdeveloped, the connections among all rural economic sectors are not as close and complicated as those among urban economic sectors, and the old system's mechanisms in the countryside are not as intricate as in the cities. In this sense, rural areas are the comparatively weak links of the old system, and they can be easily broken with few risks. Third, the farmers' great enthusiasm for production which emerged as the old system withered away expressed itself as enthusiasm for developing the commodity economy. They are making efforts to win and consolidate a status as independent commodity producers and operators, to open up diversified production and operation fields with the market as the center and create opportunities for developing the economy.

5. Speeding up market growth and promoting rural economic development.

The key to deepening the rural reform is to speed up market growth. The reform experiences over the past 10-odd years have verified that the semi-market and semi-planned "double-track system" can be adopted as a means of transition, but it can not be regarded as a long-lasting fixed system. Deepening reform and expanding the market are imperative. At present, the most important thing is to set up the fundamental structure for market growth, set up microeconomic main bodies with autonomy and encourage them to participate in equal and public competition in the market. Through the government's macro regulation, China should regulate properly the relations between economic efficiency and social justice, and between partial interests and overall interests.

To expand the market the following two main lines must be pursued:

(1) Expanding product markets. In accordance with the government's reform objectives—regulating and controlling the market and guiding enterprises by the market, the abolition of the unified and fixed state purchase and sale and the monopolized purchase and sale of agricultural products has become a must for the reform. So far, controls on about 80 percent of China's agricultural products have been lifted. Except for one or two products for which compulsory management should be carried out in view of the protection of the ecology and resources, agricultural products are mainly regulated by the market. The main problem now is that the control of some agricultural products is not thorough enough, and controls are sometimes lifted only to be put back in place later. As to the guiding ideology, China still believes that when products are sufficiently abundant market regulation should be adopted, but when there is a shortage of supply administrative planning means should be adopted; market regulation is not regarded as the fundamental mechanism for the commodity economy.

(2) Expanding the key elements market. This means ensuring that there is a reasonable flow of land, capital and labor.

The land market. At present, the concept of land contract rights is not clear. This is compounded by changes in population, which also result in changes in the land contract situation. As the rights and duties of the peasants who contract land are not clear, skilful farmers often can not get a proper scale of land and farmers who want to engage in nonagricultural work often can not break free from the land. To solve this difficult problem we should first make it clear that the contract responsibility system based on the household and with remuneration linked to output is the basic system for developing agriculture and is a permanent policy. Secondly, China will issue certificates for the use of land so as to guarantee the legal force of the current contract responsibility system and create the necessary conditions for land transfer. Thirdly, with the land-use certificates peasants may transfer the right to the use of land to enlarge the scale of farmed land or improve the land-use rate.

The financial market. As the ownership system is still not clear, people who depend on the land are loath to leave it, fearing that they will end up destitute. This ties up capital in less-productive areas. The most effective measure to deal with this situation is to set up a share-holding system, allowing stocks to be freely transferred within a certain scope. In this way we can maintain the integration of tangible capital and safeguard farmers' property rights. In addition, the traditional system of financing, such as loans between friends and relatives, should be encouraged, but transregional methods of financing, such as cooperative funds and banks should play the main role in making use of local capital to overcome capital shortages. We should also encourage the setting up of a system of mortgage loans so as to help rural households develop the financial market.

The labor market. The free flow of labor force is a prerequisite for rural economic development. The key to expanding the labor force market lies in the abolition by the government of various restrictions on the flow of labor force and increasing investment to expand the market so as to facilitate the flow of labor force. An abundance of labor force, in fact, is one of the major advantages of China's countryside.

(III) Step-by-Step Progress Is the Key to Success in China's Rural Reform

China's reform started in the countryside. The emancipation of the rural productive forces resulted in the creation of a huge amount of wealth, and the emancipation of the farmers' thinking paved the way for pushing forward the reform. China has always taken mobilizing the enthusiasm of all sectors as the starting point of the reform. In one sense, the original economic system restrained all sectors and links to various extents. Therefore, China's economic structural reform in almost all fields started from delegating power to lower levels and giving them more vested interests.

II. The Importance of the Rural Reform and Development to Macro Stability

(I) Agriculture Is the Most Important Basic Sector of China's National Economy

Food is the primary necessity of any people, and for a country like China with 1.2 billion people feeding the population is the most onerous task. The bulk of China's population are peasants, so the social situation in the rural areas has a great impact on the development of the national economy and society as a whole. Since 1978 China has practiced economic structural reform of historical significance, with the reform of the land-use system in the countryside as guidance. In the practice of rural reform China has gradually set up a series of basic policies, such as that of the contract responsibility system based on the household and with remuneration linked to output and the setting up of a two-tier operation system connecting unification with decentralization. Other economic sectors are encouraged to develop appropriately, with the public economy as the mainstay. The principle of distribution according to work is followed, with other distribution forms as supplements. Some people and certain regions are allowed to get rich first through honest labor and legal operations, with common prosperity as the objective. At the same time active steps are being taken to develop a diversified economy while guaranteeing the increase of grain output and encouraging and guiding township enterprises to develop healthily. Science, technology and education are regarded as the pillars of agricultural advance, and scientific and technical personnel are encouraged to go to the countryside to help the progress in agriculture. On the financial side, an agricultural investment system is being set up, integrating the resources of the state, collectives and farmers. Reform of the circulation system of agricultural products is being carried out in the direction of multi-channel circulation. But while all this is going on, the poverty-stricken and ethnic-minority areas are not being neglected; they are being encouraged to develop their economies using their own advantages and become better off.

So long as we develop agriculture well we can have a solid foundation for the development of the national economy. The building of the market economic system can in no way shake agriculture's basic position in the nation's economy. As early as in 1990 Comrade Deng Xiaoping pointed out: "We should always tightly grasp the issue of agriculture. It is easy for rural areas to get rich or to become poor. Agriculture will be finished if we can not till the land well."

Keeping social stability in the countryside is a matter of concern to the overall stability of China's politics and economy. The most important task for stabilizing the countryside is to develop the rural productive forces and improve the farmers' livelihoods. The latter is of direct significance for realizing the objectives of China's economic development, especially in the current situation in which agricultural development has seriously lagged behind. We can alleviate the pressure of inflation, satisfy social demand and keep social stability only through getting bumper harvests and increasing the supply of agricultural products. Moreover, we can prepare sufficient raw materials for the secondary and tertiary industries and the daily-expanding market only through bumper harvests, thus supporting the sustained, rapid and healthy development of the national economy.

To a country with a population of over one billion and comparatively little land, grain is an important issue concerning the nation's existence. So we must attach great importance to it. However, we must guard against any misunderstanding of this issue. Some foreign experts have forecast that in the middle of the next century China will be short of 370 million tons of grain. At that time, China will have exhausted its own sources of grain, and the world market will not have enough surplus grain to make up the shortfall. Hence, the question arises: Who will feed the Chinese people? The reply is: China will feed the Chinese people by itself. We shall by no means pose any such problem to the rest of the world. We shall import some grain, but mainly to stabilize grain prices on the domestic market. But China will definitely not import as much grain as 370 million tons. We must have faith in the revolution of science and technology, the progress of the socialist economic system, and the people's creativeness under the socialist market economic system with Chinese characteristics. The most important thing is to create conditions for the future development of agricultural production in a down-to-earth manner. Grain production relies not only on certain material conditions, but also on certain social conditions. We must prepare these conditions well; the way to do so is none other than by accelerating the reform and opening to the outside world.

About 80 percent of China's population of 1.2 billion is located in the countryside. Without rural development there can be no prosperity for the farmers, and no development and prosperity for China as a whole. In fact, without stable rural areas there can be no stability for the country, and the key to a stable and prosperous countryside is the raising of the farmers' enthusiasm to work in their own interests.

We should clearly realize that, though we have made great achievements in the rural economic reform and rural economic development, the reform and development are not in balance among different regions and between the countryside and the cities. Meanwhile, due to diversified consumer demands which have not led to corresponding changes in the production structure, new contradictions between supply and demand have emerged. In addition, experience in the past few years has demonstrated that China must do more in the future to better protect, support, and plan for agriculture. Policies and measures meant to narrow the gap between the income of urban and rural residents must be followed completely. There are similar economic disparities between developed and underdeveloped regions. If these gaps continue to widen grave consequences will result.

(II) Seeking Macro Stability While Coordinating Conflicting Urban and Rural Interests

The building of the socialist market economic system requires a stable social environment. Practice over the past few years has shown that only if agriculture is consolidated and the countryside remains stable can the whole nation be stable, can the economic system transition carry on smoothly and can the national economy make sustained, rapid and healthy development. Experience has also shown that it is very difficult to always give priority to rural development while making macroeconomic decisions. In special circumstances we have to sacrifice some rural interests and slow down the pace of rural reform in exchange for a short-term macroeconomic balance. Such problems are the roots of a series of issues for which decisions are very difficult to make during the transformation of China's economic system.

Fundamentally, this contradiction stems from the old planned economy system. In the past, we gave priority to the development of heavy industry. Hence we had to maintain a high rate of accumulation with a low income level. This involved keeping wages as low as possible, and this entailed lowering the prices of agricultural products which are the raw materials for food and most light industries. In this sense, the unified and fixed state purchase and marketing of agricultural products at low prices was the cornerstone of the planned economic system as a whole. When the rural reform exceeds the stage of giving the rural inhabitants enough to eat and wear and heads toward the market economy system, the original system and its macro balance mechanisms are shaken to the foundations. However, cities with the state-owned economic sector as the mainstay lag far behind the countryside, where the non-state-owned economy plays the leading role in terms of reform. There is no way for industry and commerce with low marketization levels to digest smoothly agricultural products with high marketization levels. In retrospect, since the mid-1980s we have worked on the imbalance between urban and rural reform. The dilemma is that if China speeds up the marketization of agricultural products the urban system will hardly be able to bear the strain, but if it slows down the rural reform it will be difficult to increase farmers' incomes and maintain their enthusiasm for production.

A more difficult problem is that the whole set of policy tools for maintaining the original system's macro balance has been deformed and lost its effectiveness, and the new regulation me-

CHAPTER I PERFECTING MACROECONOMIC POLICIES

chanisms based on macro control of the market economy are still to be set up. During the transformation of the economic system, once the contradictions between urban and rural interests become prominent we can neither get help from completely unified state purchase and marketing and rural isolation, nor rely on fine tuning of the market mechanisms.

The core problem we confront at the moment is not whether more macro stability is needed or if more market-oriented rural and urban reform is required. Moreover, if reform in the rural and urban areas is out of step how can we find a balanced solution to a series of difficult problems so as to reach overall stability?

III. China's Rural Problems and Agricultural Policies

(I) The Slow Increase of Peasants' Income, the Enlargement of Income Differences Between Urban and Rural Areas and Between Regions, and Grain Prices Have Become Prominent Contradictions in the Countryside

1. Stagnant or fluctuating incomes in rural areas have given birth to grave financial burden problems.

Before 1984 rural residents' incomes grew rapidly, but between 1984 and 1988 it slowed down remarkably. Between 1989 and 1991 the annual growth rate of peasants' net income per capita stood at only 0.7 percent, allowing for price rises. As the growth rate was so low that various fund reserves and collections became heavy burdens to farmers, the relations between them and government officials were strained, thus affecting the stability of political power of the grass-roots level. This was more marked in central and western China than in eastern China. Statistics show that between 1985 and 1990 farmers' actual incomes decreased in three provinces of the nine provinces and municipalities in eastern China while in 16 provinces and autonomous regions of the 21 provinces and autonomous regions in central and western China.

Peasants' burdens reflect the distribution relations among the

29

state, the collectives and individual farmers. The taxes and other fees imposed on the farmers should be spelled out in laws and contracts, but in reality units of all levels have milked the agriculture sector, greatly hampering production.

The financial burden on the farmers mainly consists of taxes paid to the state, allocations for the reserve funds of the collectives and various other fees. The total amount of taxes collected in the rural areas has been increasing year by year, as have farmers' contributions to the reserve funds, which are used to finance overall planning and labor services. On top of all this there is a wide variety of apportioned charges for such things as management fees and various fines. Rural inhabitants complain bitterly about this financial burden; reducing it will not only ensure that the rural economy achieves sustained development, it will also alleviate social contradictions, and guarantee social stability and unity.

2. The widening of the income disparity among regions has led to a large-scale migration of rural labor.

According to statistics, in 1994 some 80 million farmers left the land and moved to other parts of the country. Traditionally, Chinese peasants were most unwilling to move away from their homes, but the growing income disparity between the urban and rural areas is forcing many of them to move to other places to seek a higher standard of living. The concerned information indicates that before 1985 the growth of income and consumer levels of rural residents exceeded that of urban residents. In 1978 the income ratio between urban and rural residents was 2.4:1, and the consumption ratio between them, 2.9:1. These figures shrank to 1.7:1 and 2.2:1, respectively, in 1985. After 1985 the income growth rate of rural residents was lower than that of urban residents. In 1993 the income ratio between urban and rural residents was 2.5:1. The relative decline of peasants' consumer level is more obvious. The statistical data indicate that after 1989, the consumer ratio between urban and rural residents reached 3.2:1.

While the income disparity between urban and rural areas was growing, the disparity in farmers' incomes between eastern and central China, and between eastern and western China also widened. In 1978 the income ratio of rural residents per capita between eastern and central China was 1.25:1; and between eastern and western China, 1.26:1. The income ratio of urban residents per capita between eastern and central China, and that between eastern and western China were almost the same. In 1992 the two ratios were respectively 1.89:1 and 1.62:1. The disparity is even larger if an advanced province is compared to a backward province. For instance, in 1993 the annual income per capita in rural areas was 19.7 percent of that of Beijing, 16.2 percent of that of Shanghai and 15 percent of that of Guangdong. In addition, the income disparity between rural people who have gone to work in cities and those still working in rural areas is very large, with the latter's incomes being only 23.6 percent of those of the former. But this migration puts a strain on the household registration system and urban infrastructure facilities. The migrants have no job security, and may be sent back to their hometowns in the countryside at any time. In addition, many of them cannot find jobs in the cities immediately, and this gives rise to social problems. Some people maintain that farmers should be restricted to the land so as not to cause problems in the cities. But this is obviously not a solution to the problem of income disparity.

3. The Grain Issue.

It is indeed amazing that China supports 22 percent of the world's total population with only seven percent of the world's total arable land. However, such a tremendous achievement has not changed China's basic conditions that arable land per capita is much lower than the world's average. Moreover, along with economic development, China's arable land will continue to decrease, while the demand for grain, especially for forage grain, will increase by a large margin. As a big country with one fourth of the world's population, it is impossible for China to mainly rely on grain imports to meet the demand. Grain prices rose sharply in 1993 and 1994, which attracted nationwide attention. It seems that the fluctuation of grain prices has become an indicator of imminent crisis.

THE REFORM AND DEVELOPMENT OF CHINA'S RURAL ECONOMY

When analyzing the issue of China's agriculture, we must trace back to the end of the 1980s:

First, sharp fluctuations in economic growth caused the external environment for agriculture to deteriorate.

The year 1988 witnessed the most serious inflation in China since the initiation of the reform: Prices increased by 18.5 percent over the previous year (becoming 11.2 percent higher than in the previous year). Starting in autumn 1988, the Chinese government began to improve and rectify the economy. Guided by the policy of controlling economic growth, China's economy developed at a low speed. The GDP growth rate decreased from 11.3 percent in 1988 to 4.3 percent in 1989, and to 3.9 percent in 1990. In these two years the average annual industrial growth rate was only 4.2 percent, and the average annual growth rate of the construction industry decreased by 3.7 percent. However, the average annual growth rate of agriculture (crop cultivation) reached 5.9 percent. Within the two years the output of grain, cotton and edible oil increased respectively by 13.2 percent, 8.7 percent and 22.2 percent, but due to sluggish demand the prices of agricultural products declined with the increase of their output. For example, in 1991 the purchase price of grain shrank by 12.6 percent compared to 1989, and this meant that farmers' incomes did not increase even after bumper harvests.

In 1991 the economy began to pick up again. In 1992 and 1993 the average annual growth rate of the GDP reached 13.5 percent, that of industry as a whole stood at 21.4 percent and that of the construction industry, at 18.0 percent. This round of rapid economic growth, with the rapid expansion of the investment scale of capital construction as the main engine, brought about the outflow of a great deal of key agricultural production elements. The years 1992 and 1993 witnessed arable land shrink by 4.147 million *mu* (1 *mu*=1/15 ha) annually on average. In fact, the annual average occupation of arable land was 11.038 million *mu*, 13.2 times the average annual shrinkage between 1989 and 1991. Of the state's total investment in capital construction, the investment in agriculture decreased from 4.0 percent in 1991 to 2.8 percent in 1993.

CHAPTER I PERFECTING MACROECONOMIC POLICIES

The above figures indicate that sharp fluctuations in economic growth do not benefit agriculture: Too low an economic growth rate will lead to sluggish demand, a fall in the prices of agricultural products, and no increase in farmers' incomes even after bumper harvests. On the other hand, too speedy economic development will siphon off key elements of agricultural production and cause agriculture to stagnate. Hence, the prime requirement for stable agriculture is a stable economic environment as a whole.

Second, new difficulties have arisen for farmers in seeking more job openings and increasing their incomes.

In any country the prosperity or otherwise of agriculture is related to two aspects, i.e., the supply of agricultural products and the increase of farmers' incomes. The conditions in China are even more special: The population in the countryside is huge, so farmers can hardly depend only on increases in agricultural production and the raising of prices for agricultural products for an increase in their incomes. In the mid-1980s farmers' incomes increased mainly because many rural laborers found jobs in non-agricultural sectors. Between 1984 and 1988, 63.11 million rural laborers were employed by township enterprises—an annual average of 12.622 million, equivalent to 117.4 percent of the average annual increase of rural laborers in the same period. Between 1989 and 1993 township enterprises employed 19.112 million more people, which was an annual average increase of 3.822 million, equivalent to 45.6 percent of the average annual increase of rural laborers. Because of fewer job opportunities in the rural areas and sustained low prices for agricultural products before October 1993 there was a sharp rise in the number of farmers migrating to cities. During this period, farmers' net income per capita increased by only 2.23 percent annually on average. Even in 1994, when the prices of agricultural products rose by a large margin, their net income per capita grew by only five percent. In the past six years the average annual growth rate of farmers' net income per capita has been only 2.7 percent.

In light of the overall development in the rural areas, the main contradiction and most prominent issue now is the reform of the land-use system.

In the 1980s the reform of most profound significance to the rural areas was the adoption of the household contract responsibility system with remuneration linked to output. This separated the land-use right from the operation right. Giving peasants the operation right has greatly stimulated their enthusiasm for production, thus greatly improving the land's output level. In recent years, in light of the new conditions of rural reform, the term for contracting land has been extended. The right to the use of land is allowed to be transferred in accordance with the law. However, these measures, though positive, have not fundamentally solved the question of land property rights.

The amount of land taken up for non-agricultural uses has grown steadily, the area on which grain is grown has shrunk correspondingly and the gap between land supply and demand has widened. One of the reasons for this has been the craze for setting up "development zones."

In the past few years land readjustment in many areas has been more frequent, with shorter and shorter intermissions due to changes in population and the sequestering of land for non-agricultural purposes.

The input (including labor, capital and technology) into agriculture has declined, and in particular investment by farmers in land has remarkably decreased, as the problem of short-term planning has become more prominent in the rural areas. In the past two years the input into agriculture has got constantly smaller. In 1994 the country's investment in agriculture dropped from 2.8 percent to 2.2 percent compared to the previous year.

The basis of agricultural development and rural stability is land. In the course of deepening the rural reform and speeding up rural marketization, China must be bolder in carrying out the reform of the land-use system in the countryside and lay a solid foundation for rural property rights.

The rural contradictions which are prominent at present and are expected to linger for a fairly long time to come are as follows:

The contradiction between household small production and

CHAPTER I PERFECTING MACROECONOMIC POLICIES

the development of the market economy. The small-scale peasant economy is the main aspect of the contradiction, which keeps the current rural economy in China still at the level of the self-sufficient natural economy. The nature of such small-scale peasant economy in the countryside is not decided by the household operation form, but by the land system of equally dividing the land into small pieces and carrying out monopolized operation. A large number of people are forced to work on scattered small plots, a fact which has given China difficulty in reforming the means and forms of agricultural production, and has sent agriculture into a serious decline. This will continue to be the main obstacle to agricultural development in the future.

Circulation and production are out of step with each other. Thanks to the rural economic reform, peasants now have autonomy of production, and rural households engage in independent production and accumulation. With such autonomy farmers now have control over the products of their labor. Therefore, setting up and perfecting the market system in the countryside, creating the most favorable environment for rational circulation and the best setup for the elements of production, and promoting the further development of agricultural production are tasks that brook no delay.

Channeling the surplus labor force in the countryside into non-agricultural economic sectors will be the focus of the rural reform for quite a long time to come as well as presenting the main contradiction in the rural economic development. How to raise rural productivity to a new level to make the farmers well off is where the key to further rural reform lies. With the development of the commodity economy, the emergence of a large amount of surplus labor force, a restriction on rural economic growth, has hindered the rural areas from adopting advanced technologies and achieving large-scale economic returns.

Coordinating the relations between urban and rural areas has become an important task. The contradictions between the new and old systems mainly reflect the contradictions between urban and rural areas. The problems that appear in purchasing grain and in circulation are due to the fact that the cities are used to the old methods of getting products to take care of the interests of the urban population and industry. As the rural reform progresses, urban reform must be coordinated with it, and the interests of urban and rural areas, of peasants and workers, must be regulated. When township enterprises move forward, the exchanges and mutual help between urban and rural areas must be strengthened, and the relations between township enterprises and major industries in cities should be readjusted. As agricultural production grows China should readjust the prices for agricultural products to mobilize peasants' enthusiasm for production, increase agricultural output, improve the conditions for production and raise the output per unit of land. However all these involve strategic planning for urban and rural areas, and for agriculture and industry.

The contradictions between the demands of urban and rural people for improving their material lives and the backward agricultural productivity and between the supply of and demand for agricultural and sideline products are the main contradictions in the present stage of the reform in the countryside. In view of the current consumption structure, incessant rise of the consumption level and population growth, it can be estimated that shortages of agricultural and sideline products will be a general trend for quite a long period of time.

(II) Optimizing Macroeconomic Policies to Suit Market Orientation of Agricultural Products and Avoid the Trend Toward Urbanization

1. There is not much leeway for readjusting agricultural policies.

While working out policies for agriculture three related aspects must be considered simultaneously: First, the agricultural policies should not harm the stability of the economy as a whole. Otherwise China will seek temporary relief regardless of the consequences and will finally harm both agriculture and the peasants. Second, the formulation of agricultural policies must effectively promote the stable growth of the supply of basic agricultural products. Third, the working out of agricultural

CHAPTER I PERFECTING MACROECONOMIC POLICIES

policies must help to provide rural laborers with jobs and increase farmers' incomes. It is not hard to see that it is very difficult to handle properly the relations among the three aspects. If China can not transfer surplus labor force from rural areas or make the prices of agricultural products rational, it will be hard to raise farmers' incomes. However, if China transfers rural labor force on a fairly large scale and raises the prices of agricultural products by a comparatively large margin, it will require a higher speed of economic growth to avoid adding fuel to inflation. This shows that the margin for readjusting agricultural policies is not wide enough. We may even say that with the original structure and within the original structure frame, there is not much room for China to readjust its agricultural policies. Therefore, the only way out is to further reform the existing economic system and structure.

Since 1990 new fluctuations in and slow growth of farmers' incomes have aroused great attention from the central government. In recent years the central government has held three rural work meetings in succession, clearly putting forward the two major strategic tasks confronting China's agriculture and rural economy—guaranteeing the effective supply of agricultural products and increasing peasants' incomes; and two objectives to be achieved by the end of this century—grain output of 1,000 billion *jin* (1 *jin*=0.5 kg) and farmers' living standards to reach the "well-off" level (annual per capita income of RMB 1,100 yuan calculated at 1990 prices). For this, the central government has worked out a series of policies and measures for strengthening agriculture and the rural economy in the following five aspects:

First, further stabilize and perfect the basic system of the rural economy to protect and mobilize farmers' activities. The Chinese government has reiterated that the contract responsibility system based on the household with remuneration linked to output and the dual-layer operation system will not change for quite a long time to come, and pointed out definitely that upon the expiration of the original 15-year contract term, the term will be extended for another 30 years. And within the contract period the principle of "no increase in the land when the number of family members grows; and no decrease in the land when the number of family members declines" be adopted. The right to the use of the land may be transferred at farmers' will and with compensation, on the premise of no changes in the ownership or application of the land. Rural collective organizations are encouraged to run economic entities through the share-holding system and other forms of cooperation.

Second, rural reform will be deepened and a rural economic system should be set up tallying with the market economy. This should include promotion of reform of the purchase and sales system for grain and other major agricultural products, the development of rural markets for key elements of production and the acceleration of reform of township enterprises.

Third, solve the problems in agricultural development and give strong support to grain and cotton production. It has been decided that the government will allocate RMB 6.5 billion yuan of interest-deducted loans every year to support economic development in 500-odd large grain-producing counties and over 150 major cotton-producing counties.

Fourth, develop the rural economy in an all-round way to increase farmers' incomes. China will continue to encourage the rational readjustment of the agricultural production structure by allocating loans of RMB one billion yuan every year to develop the "high-yield, fine-quality and high-efficiency" exemplary agricultural counties. Every year the government also allocates special loans of RMB 10 billion yuan to develop township enterprises in central and western China.

Fifth, increase investment in agriculture and improve its comprehensive production capability. The Chinese government has decided to readjust the distribution structure of the national income, and raise the income within the financial budget and the proportions of the state's investment in capital construction and credit capital for use in agriculture. It has also specified that the growth rate of its total financial input into agriculture should be higher than the growth rate of normal financial income, and the growth rate of agricultural loans should be two percent higher than the average growth rate of various loans.

CHAPTER I PERFECTING MACROECONOMIC POLICIES

The main contradiction in the rural economic structural reform is that the macroeconomic system and the policy-related environment do not conform to the microeconomic base. Along with the founding of the rural double-layer operation system with the contract responsibility system based on the household and with remuneration linked to output as the mainstay, the highly centralized planning and management system in the countryside has been gradually transferred into one with market orientation as the mainstay and the objective of winning maximum profits as the motive power. Hence, the farmers' income level was raised again by a large margin after 1984. Meanwhile, large amounts of capital, labor force and other production elements have flowed to the secondary and tertiary industries, and agricultural production has suffered from setbacks due to insufficient investment. In addition, the phenomenon of farmers' income decreasing with the growth of output has appeared in the rural economy for the first time. In essence, such a phenomenon mainly results from the coexistence of the two types of systems which simultaneously play roles in economic activities. If the microeconomic main body is more active, the internal impulse of development will be stronger, and it will be more difficult to keep a balance between the size and structure of the national economy based on the original economic system. So when contradictions accumulate to a certain degree, the government has to adopt various compulsory measures to restore the balance. Between 1989 and 1991 the output of grain and other agricultural products increased by a large margin, and farmers' actual incomes dropped sharply for the second time, a fact which should be attributed to bureaucratic interference. The problems that we are confronted with now are clashes and contradictions between the traditional macro system and the microeconomic main body touched off by the policy-related environment and reform. The essence of these contradictions lies in the clashes and confrontations between farmers' internal motives for obtaining maximum profits and an irrational economic framework.

2. Macroeconomic policies should benefit the coordination of urban and rural interests.

39

THE REFORM AND DEVELOPMENT OF CHINA'S RURAL ECONOMY

Another important characteristic of the rural economic reform in the 1990s is that it has started to break down the barriers between agriculture and industry, and between the cities and the countryside. Experience has shown that the rural reform is becoming more and more closely connected with the urban reform. For instance, millions of peasants work in the cities. They are active in the urban market of agricultural products, contract projects in urban areas and build up small towns by themselves.

To lift controls from the prices of agricultural products, including grain and cotton, and speed up the realization of fixing the prices of agricultural products according to the market are the keys to the rural economic reform. We should say that the guiding ideology on this issue is clear. In 1985 the central government proclaimed the abolition of planned purchase and marketing by the state. In the early 1990s the state lifted controls from the purchase prices of grain and edible oil, worked out the purchase protection and guiding prices of wheat and rice, adopted the highest prices for agricultural means of production, and increased the purchase prices for grain and cotton in accordance with contracts. All these measures have played healthy roles in stabilizing agricultural production, increasing agricultural incomes and mobilizing farmers' enthusiasm.

However, as the problem affects the national situation as a whole and has a direct impact on the interests of cities, the contradictions between urban and rural interests caused by the purchase and marketing of grain and cotton in the past two years have become prominent, even very sharp in some regions. With a gradually awakened sense of the market, farmers take the market as guidance for their production and sales, and regard the pursuit of maximum profits as their chief objective. Moreover, due to excessively rapid increases in agricultural costs and excessively low purchase prices for agricultural products, the phenomenon of "waiting for the right price to sell" has become common. The government finds itself in a dilemma: On the one hand, it encourages farmers to increase their incomes in accordance with the market demand; and on the other, to protect the production, purchase and marketing of grain and cotton, which give comparatively low economic returns but are of great importance for the national economy and people's livelihood. When it is impossible to give consideration to both aspects, the government often shows more concern about the quantity of agricultural products which peasants can supply to maintain the cities' stability. To obtain instant results the government will adopt familiar administrative means to reinforce traditional operations and weaken the market function. When supplies of grain and cotton are insufficient the government will force farmers to grow more grain. Once there is a bumper harvest the government will purchase grain and cotton at low prices, or even take a laissez-faire attitude. So farmers must take some self-protection measures, such as by reducing input into agriculture and giving up farming to do business, in pursuit of comparatively high economic returns.

Practice has shown that, though it is a common understanding that the control of the prices of agricultural products must be lifted completely, the government's macro policies and macro-control measures for the rural economy can not be solidly founded on the basis of the market mechanism governing agricultural products without a correct balance of the interest relations between rural and urban areas. Hence, deviations will appear in practice and harm farmers' direct interests.

Two possibilities are worth studying: One is that the government can completely push agricultural products onto the market and take a thoroughgoing laissez-faire attitude. According to the general principles of economics, the changes in market prices will finally lead the flow of key elements of production, reversing the long-standing rise or decline of market prices and realizing the rational disposition of resources. However, agricultural problems have their own characteristics. The spontaneously operating market mechanisms can not completely and effectively play their full roles in agriculture. As a result, periodic fluctuations in the market mechanism are inevitable, further affecting the development of the whole national economy and social stability. The traditional planned price system impairs the interests of agriculture and the farmers, but spontaneous market pricing is also detrimental in these aspects.

The other possibility is that under the name of macro control, the government can resort to the traditional planned regulation and control methods. Consequently, when the supply of agricultural products is larger than the demand, the government pushes agricultural products onto the market, resulting in the phenomena of difficulty in selling grain and cotton. When the supply is short of the demand, the government will adopt macro control because there is difficulty in buying grain and cotton, and sends teams to rural areas for compulsory purchasing.

In deepening the rural reform it is urgent to solve the problem of coordinating the interests of the urban and rural areas and of the country and the farmers while control of the market prices of agricultural products is being lifted, so as to make the macro-control policies more practical.

We should take into account the macroeconomic policies and guiding ideologies during the course of the rural reform. The most fundamental and essential issue at present is to strengthen the government's input into agro-science research, agricultural education and the construction of agricultural infrastructure facilities. We must also readjust the proportions between industry and agriculture to keep the rural and urban interests coordinated and balanced, and make agriculture adapt to the needs of the national economy. However, the relative backwardness of agriculture is worrisome. In the past few years the scale of the state's capital construction has been large, but investment in capital construction for agriculture has fallen in successive years. If the imbalance between agricultural and industrial development continues, the basically balanced setup between supply and demand for which we have worked for many years may take a turn for the worse and cause big problems.

The key to coordinating the relations between industry and agriculture and the interests of urban and rural areas lies in increasing farmers' incomes and making the rural areas rich and prosperous. In the early days of China's industrialization, agriculture has to support industry. But after urban industry has developed and has cultivated the ability of self-accumulation, more value generated by rural areas should be left in the countryside

CHAPTER I PERFECTING MACROECONOMIC POLICIES

for creating a favorable development environment for agriculture. To keep the whole situation stable we should fully realize the importance of peasants' income to the stable growth of the domestic market and prevent any tendency to overemphasize the cities when drawing up policies.

In accordance with the demands of the market economy, only through removing the "barriers between urban and rural areas" and perfecting the macro environment can we straighten out the relation between the microeconomic and macroeconomic systems in the countryside. At present, in China the only effective way to truly increase and stabilize peasants' incomes is to constantly raise agricultural productivity. There are two concrete and effective ways of doing this: The first is to reduce the number of peasants, effectively transfer the surplus agricultural labor force to other employment and raise the amount of land cultivated per laborer. The other way is to increase the input of science and technology, and improve agriculture's abilities in production and operation. The first way is the most important. If China can effectively transfer surplus labor force from the countryside step by step, the disposition of key agricultural elements will become rational and productivity will increase constantly. Along with constant perfection of the market economy system, rural microeconomic vitality will be fully and protractedly brought into play, and rural collective, cooperative and agricultural economies of scale will gradually be strengthened and rationalized.

According to the demands of the law of market economy development, the key to deepening the rural reform is to loosen the macroeconomic system and the policy-related environment. Surplus agricultural labor force is encouraged to flow to cities in an appropriate manner, finding employment in secondary and tertiary industries. But this cannot be accomplished merely by setting up township enterprises. There are two reasons for this: a. The scale and development speed of township enterprises do not keep pace with the economic transition; and b. They only serve to increase rural people's incomes, without stimulating the internal vitality and development mechanism of agricultural production. In addition, they slow the transfer of surplus rural labor to places where it is most needed and slows the pace of urbanization in the nation as a whole. Only through lowering the "barrier between urban and rural areas," and speeding up the process of urbanization can the rural surplus labor force be effectively transferred to gradually reach the objective of economic transition, thus enabling China's agricultural production and rural economy to step onto the normal development track.

In view of the present state of China's current economy and reform, the country has the conditions for gradually lowering this barrier. First of all, the setting up of the objectives of the market economy has provided a solid theoretical base and a flexible environment for macroeconomic structural reform and the perfection of the policy-related environment. Second, thanks to efforts over the past 40-plus years, China has built up a comparatively complete industrial structure and system. Moreover, through the deepening of the reform of the economic system and the further perfection of the market mechanisms, the vitality of large and medium-sized enterprises will be further reinforced. They have the ability to develop normally by relying on their own accumulation. Third, except for a small number of large and medium-sized cities among China's 450 large cities, the rest 334 medium-sized and small cities each with a population of fewer than 300,000, have shown very low economic achievements, but have a high demand for development and huge potential. Jobless people in the cities make up 2.6 percent of the total urban population (excluding those who have voluntarily quit their jobs), or 2.4 percent lower than the internationally recognized "normal" unemployment rate of five percent. Fourth, the values of China's farmers have changed, their sense of competition and risk have been reinforced, and a large number of farmer entrepreneurs who know how to operate and manage businesses have emerged. They enter cities not only as laborers, but also as investors, business operators and managers. Fifth, the reform and opening to the outside world have done away with the unitary structure of China's ownership and distribution system, mobilized the initiative of various sectors, attracted a large amount of foreign capital and technology, and created favorable domestic and international environments involving economic growth and the readjustment of production. All of these things have opened vast prospects for the effective transfer of rural laborers and the quickening of urbanization. Therefore, we have reason to believe that improving the macro policy-related environment and lowering the "barrier between urban and rural areas" is not a matter of choice but of time and method.

3. The government's indirect role in market agricultural development.

Financial Measures The exemption from and reduction of agricultural taxes.

The production characteristics of industry and agriculture dictate that the growth of agricultural labor productivity always lags behind that of industrial labor productivity. Hence it is difficult to eliminate the long-standing large price differences between industrial and agricultural products. Instead, they will usually be aggravated. Therefore, agriculture is always in an unfavorable development position in the overall economy. To guarantee the average profits of agricultural production, the government may attempt to balance industrial and agricultural development through regulating industrial and agricultural taxes.

Financial Policies Special loans and support credit from agricultural banks.

The government must give special support to investment in agriculture, especially in areas which have an environmental or social impact, through the setting up of special banks for this purpose.

Welfare Policies The setting up of agricultural insurance bodies and rural medical insurance.

Agriculture takes the whole natural environment as its field of production. So agricultural production is threatened by natural disasters as well as economic risks. To improve farmers' ability to withstand these risks, the government should set up special bodies to insure crops.

Administrative Legislation Agricultural legislation should ensure the protection of resources, and support prices and investment in science and technology.

Agricultural Resources The steady loss of arable land makes it imperative to protect agricultural resources in order to guarantee the long-term stable growth of the national economy.

4. The demarcation of government involvement in agricultural development in the market economy.

In a market economy the dynamics of government involvement in agriculture are not without demarcation. In view of the objective demands of market economy operations, the government exerts influence on the aforementioned aspects related to agriculture and is also restrained by the marketization of agricultural product exchange, farmers' income growth, agricultural autonomy over operations, the state's financial revenue and expenditure, the growth stage of the national economy and the psychological factors among urban and rural residents.

First, the government's involvement should be demarcated so that it does not infringe upon the market mechanism governing agricultural product exchange.

Under the market economy the government's involvement in agricultural development is limited to making up the intrinsic shortcomings in market agricultural development and guaranteeing the stable development of the agricultural market. This is totally different from its role in the old planned economy system.

Second, government involvement should not hamper the growth of farmers' incomes or the increase of agricultural output.

Agricultural development is not only an issue of pure industrial development, it is also an issue related to rural development and farmers' income levels. However, the urban-rural structure and the relative shortage of agricultural resources force the government to interfere with the problems of agriculture, but farmers' income growth and the steady increase of agricultural output should not be impaired.

Third, the government should not interfere with the farmers' autonomy of operation.

Fourth, the government's support for agriculture should be demarcated by the state's financial ability.

The implementation of any policy involves interest readjustment among various principals. Hence the implementation of any policy has its own corresponding costs. However, a country's financial income is limited at any particular time. So the number of policy levers should be limited by a country's financial ability.

Fifth, the dynamics of government involvement in agriculture should be limited by the psychological preparedness of both urban and rural residents.

The effects of any agricultural policy can eventually be reflected in the behavior of various agricultural economic principals (producers and consumers). Therefore, in agricultural development the dynamics of government involvement should be demarcated by the psychological endurance of urban and rural residents.

Sixth, the government interference in agriculture should not exceed the special demands upon agriculture during the growth stage of the national economy.

As an important component of the national economy, agricultural development must be adapted to social development as a whole. In the early days of industrialization, many countries adopted the "squeeze" type of agricultural policy. However, when the lagging development of agriculture becomes a bottleneck in the national economic growth, coordinating industry and agriculture becomes the main objective of agricultural policy. Therefore, in agricultural development, government involvement should not go beyond the special demands upon agriculture during the growth stage of the national economy.

Chapter II
Rural Land System Reform

I. Problems in the Land-Use System

(I) New Ideas on Land Use Will Bring Vitality to Rural Economic Development

1. From the point of view of the development of the countryside the key problem is the land-use system.

In the 1980s the implementation of the household contract responsibility system in the countryside was an important change with far-reaching consequences. It gave the farmers the right to manage their land, and this brought their initiative for production into full play. As a result, agricultural output soared. In recent years, in line with the new situation in the countryside, the contract period has been extended and the right to use the land can be transferred in accordance with the law. But the problem of the property right of the land has not been basically solved. Therefore, land complications have become more serious in the last two years.

(1) More land is being taken up for non-agricultural use, and at the same time more land is going out of cultivation. So the grain-sown area has shrunk and the gap between grain supply and demand has been widened. This is partly because of the "development zone craze" and "real estate craze." In the last two years, as much as ten million *mu* of land has been lost, and now the average arable land per capita is less than one *mu* in one third of China's provinces and autonomous regions. In order to guarantee grain production, the minimum sown area can not be less than 1,650 million *mu*. But in 1992 the sown area had shrunk to 1,660 *mu*, very close to the minimum. In 1993 another 1.1 million *mu* had been lost. In 1994 the grain-sown area had been further

CHAPTER II RURAL LAND SYSTEM REFORM

reduced in 19 provinces and autonomous regions, and as a result, the sown area was only 1,640 million *mu* in that year. At present, the average arable land per capita in China is only 1.2 *mu*, one fourth of the world's average.

(2) The land is readjusted frequently and randomly.

The present policies include the stipulation that the ownership of the land belongs to the collective, and that the household contract responsibility system should be consolidated and perfected. The first 15-year contract period can be extended by a further 30 years. During this period the relations between the contracting parties is not to be adjusted simply because of the changes in the number of people involved. Compensated transfer of contracted land is permitted. The present area of land responsibility is distributed according to the population. So, in order to solve the land problem brought about by the changes in the number of people the land must be redistributed objectively. In the last two years many places have frequently readjusted the land because of population changes and the extension of non-agricultural use of land. The policy of small adjustments by the central government becomes the basis for their readjustment. But these "small changes," if frequent enough, may affect the implementation of the responsibility system and the expected results of farmers' investment.

(3) The input (including labor, capital and technology) into agriculture has decreased, especially the input into land, from farm households.

The state's investment in agriculture decreased to 2.2 percent in 1994 from 2.8 percent in the previous year. Investment by the farmers themselves is very important, but only real benefits can attract their input. In the last two years the investment enthusiasm of the peasants has been lowered because of influence of the unclear land property rights and the low benefits from grain production. The funds which should have been invested in agricultural production have been used for non-agricultural purposes. Furthermore, many qualified farmers and technicians have transferred to non-agricultural jobs. Land is the basis of agricultural production and economic stability. In the process of deepening the rural reform and quickening the pace of marketization we have to be bold in reforming the rural land-use system and lay a solid foundation for solving the problem of property rights in the countryside.

2. The present land system's influence on the farmers.

In upholding the policy of the land belonging to the collective, it often happens that the higher-level authorities, in the name of the owner, come to infringe upon the peasants' right to use and profit from land. From the establishment of the people's communes in 1958 to the present contract responsibility system the arrangement of property rights under collective land ownership has experienced several changes in methods of decision making and distribution. Before the reform the three-level system of ownership (people's commune, production brigade and production team) with the production team as the basic form was practiced in the rural area. At that time, though the production team had the right to use the land and distribute the profits, the higher-level authorities controlled the grain crop and often collected money or grain from the surplus income. But even since the introduction of the household contract responsibility system, though the farmers have more rights over the disposition of the land and their surplus income they still can not refuse to pay arbitrary charges imposed on them by the higher authorities, which has dampened their enthusiasm for farming.

The collective ownership of the land is made clear in the land distribution rules. Before the reform every person who was a member of a collective had the right to enjoy collective earnings from the land. Under the household responsibility system each member of the collective can share the right to use the land. So the land was distributed on a per capita basis when the responsibility system was introduced in the countryside. This means that every newborn legal member also has the right to share the land. That is why many places in the countryside have redistributed the land, which contradicts the central government policy of a 15-year unchangeable contract period. According to a sample survey of 300 villages, 65.2 percent had readjusted their contracted land since the carrying out of the responsibility system. And

CHAPTER II RURAL LAND SYSTEM REFORM

in most of these cases the reason was population change.

The following problems occur: a) Owing to the redistribution of the land according to the changing number of people involved, the farmers do not know whether they will be able to keep the land they originally contracted. This discourages them from making long-term investments in the land; b) Because of the differences in the quality and quantity of the land it has to be divided up into many small pieces in order to give each person an equal share. This also discourages investment in the land; c) Each redistribution involves an inconvenient and expensive survey of the size of population and area of land; d) In fact there are differences among the households in their agricultural input of funds and labor, which have been manifested since <u>the implementation of the responsibility system, and the equal distribution of the land has hampered the economical and effective use of the land, which is scarce in China.</u>

The purpose of the implementation of the household contract responsibility system is to set the peasants minds at ease and encourage them to invest more in the land to increase the agricultural output rate. The state has stressed the stability of this policy, but it is sometimes in conflict with the proper arrangement of land resources and limits the management of the land to the household scale. This problem has been demonstrated clearly in the Pearl River Delta, where secondary and tertiary industries have developed rapidly, giving a boost to encroachment on arable land. The result has been that land-use rights have been put on the market and the prices for such rights have soared. So the farmers consider their land a valuable commodity, and are not willing to accept the overall arrangement and unified planning for the proper use of the land. This in turn hampers the industrialization and urbanization of the countryside, integration of town and country and the present modernization trend.

3. Only the reform of the land-use right can rekindle the farmers' enthusiasm and lay a solid foundation for solving the other problems in the countryside at the present stage.

The land system includes various arrangements and regulations for land aimed at encouraging its productive use. Under the condition of collective ownership it is important to make a clear distinction between the various types of property right, straighten out the relations between ownership and use right, and standardize behavior as regards the various types of property right. All of these have a direct influence on the utilization rate of the land.

The unclear nature of land property right and frequent changes of management right are the main obstacles hampering investment by the farmers in the land. Land ownership is still not clear, land-use rights not stable and land management in chaos under the present land system. So the farmers are reluctant to invest in their land, especially on a medium- or long-term basis because of changes in the management right of the land. Therefore, in order to solve these problems the present land-use system has to be reformed.

In recent years the rural economy has developed slowly because of the delay in the reform of the land system, slowing the development of rural productivity.

(II) The Law Should Guarantee the Farmers' Long-Term Land-Use Rights

From 1979 to 1983 land was distributed equally by grade and according to the population size. But following changes in the rural population most of the townships and villages have redistributed their land. There are two types of adjustment: small-scale and large-scale. Small-scale adjustment refers to the adjustments made only in the families which have changes in the numbers of their family members, which may happen every few years. The families which do not have such changes are not included, and their land area remains unchanged.

Large-scale adjustment refers to the redistribution of the land of all the families in a village. The land is first returned to the collective and then redistributed according to the number of members in each family. So each household may get a different piece of land. Large-scale adjustment can take place every three to six years.

Long-term input is one of the standards by which to judge the stability of the land-use right. About 60 percent of households

CHAPTER II RURAL LAND SYSTEM REFORM

have not made any long-term input in their land in the more than a decade since the disintegration of the collective farms. The other households have only gone so far as to use organic fertilizer. Statistics show that 83 percent of farmers want permanent land-use right, and say that if they had it they would consider long-term investment in the land, such as terracing slopes, leveling fields, digging wells, increasing irrigation facilities, applying more organic fertilizer and planting trees.

Even though the central government has explicitly stipulated that the land contract period will be extended for another 30 years many farmers are still not confident about the stability of land use and long-term expectations for the land. Therefore, it would be better to affirm longer-term or permanent land-use rights through legislation. In this way, the various land rights and interests of farm households, such as use, transfer, rent and inheritance, will be clearly defined and protected by law, and the farmers' initiative for long-term development of their land will be brought into play.

(III) Changing the Land System Needs Caution Because It Is Closely Related to Rural Development

The comprehensive output rate of agriculture which is used to judge China's present agricultural growth is closely related to, but not exclusively so, the design and operational state of the arable land system. The system poses complicated problems, which include property right, distribution, circulation and renting of the land, operational form, and land tax and land management systems.

From history we can easily find that if increase in agricultural production is connected merely with a specific farm land policy, this leads to errors in both theory and practice.

The large-scale agricultural system which mixed up the two problems of management scale and organizational form was once popular all over the world. Besides the former Soviet Union and China, Peru, Ecuador, Bolivia, Tanzania, Guyana and some other countries also established collective farms owned by the state or by collectives. The theory was that this was the best way to improve agricultural technologies and agricultural labor productivity. But the result was that agriculture deteriorated because of the underemployment of peasants and the low efficiency and expensive management of the farms. But can the household responsibility system guarantee better results? Not necessarily.

In some South Asian countries, such as India, Pakistan and Bangladesh, farms are traditionally managed by households, and they have gained a great deal of experience, especially in intensive agricultural strategy. But they have not achieved very good results as far as agricultural productivity increase is concerned. The main reason is the dispersed property rights to land, which is not conducive to developing the market or to fund accumulation. A recent investigation in Peru and Nicaragua showed that the household farming system which was implemented in these countries in the 1980s stimulated the peasants' enthusiasm, reduced management and supervision costs and increased operation efficiency. But because there was no risk-sharing mechanism nor enough non-agricultural employment opportunities the fields were taken back by the collectives and agricultural production stagnated.

Agricultural growth is also affected by other policies and environmental factors besides the above-mentioned farmland system, such as agricultural trade conditions, non-agricultural sector growth, employment opportunities, population increase, manpower and capital input and the improvement of agricultural technologies.

We should make it clear that agricultural growth and rural development are two different concepts. The former only demonstrates the raising of the comprehensive output rate of agriculture while rural development includes fair income distribution in the course of agricultural increase, the rising prosperity of the majority of peasants, rural social civilization and overall improvement of the countryside. In the past 20 years the focus of studies and policymaking in the developing countries has gradually shifted to "development" from "growth."

To measure China's agricultural growth at the present stage, the comprehensive output rate of agriculture is the proper yardstick. The factors affecting the raising of the comprehensive output rate of agriculture can not only be found in the farmland system but also in other aspects of agriculture, as mentioned above. In order to harmonize agricultural growth and rural development, attention should also be paid to the creation of non-agricultural employment opportunities and the problems of urban and rural circulation and coordination.

At the same time, entrenching the household responsibility system is not enough to bring into being a system in agriculture that encourages innovation and allows for flexible adjustment while ensuring stability. We should study the new problems and new conditions that have appeared during the carrying out of the household responsibility system to promote the development of agriculture to a new stage.

II. Land Circulation and Scale Management

(I) Establishing an Effective Circulation Mechanism Is the Key to the Construction of the Farmland System

1. The change of the rural economic structure has put great demands on circulation and regrouping.

The basic characteristics of the farmland system are as follows: collective ownership, household contract system, two-tier management and socialized services. Under the condition of collective ownership, the household contract system has basically realized the integration of the laborer and his means of production, and solved the problem of "eating out of the same big pot." The goal of the implementation of two-tier management and socialized services is to solve the problems and difficulties caused by small-scale household management. Socialized services include the following aspects: 1) Services which are beyond the ability of, or not worthwhile for, one family are supplied by the collective; 2) The adjustment of land for farm households is done by the collective. This system gives full play to the advantages of small-scale land management and makes possible the gradual increase of agricultural production with the existing productive forces. However, problems of land circulation have appeared.

First, collective adjustment has met with some resistance and the transfer of contracted land among farm households is limited. According to the present regulations, if a household does not want to till its plot, the land can be returned to the collective for adjustment or transfer directly to another household. But in many places such adjustment is done informally, due to the lack of an official mechanism.

Second, the more services the peasants get from the collective the more they want to keep their land. Some places which have better economic strength enjoy "five unified" services or "six unified" services (unified planting plan; unified purchasing, management and use of large and medium-sized farming machinery; unified planning and farmland capital construction; unified machine plowing and seeding; unified purchasing of chemical fertilizer and pesticide; and unified arrangement of industry and sideline occupations). The key links in agricultural production are mainly handled by the collective. Most of services supplied by the collective are inexpensive and some are even free of charge. In this way production costs are reduced for the farmers, but the actual cost is very high. The collective uses the profits for agricultural production. There is no doubt that this is an important measure to guarantee agricultural development under the condition of exchange of unequal values of industrial and agricultural products and distorted grain and oil prices. Since the peasants can make profits from their contracted land, why should they give it up? For this reason, some people who are engaged in other occupations and are not interested in farming still do not want to return their land to the collective or transfer it to other households.

The above phenomenon is a complicated economic and social problem. First, the formulation of a system is the result of the development of the productive forces and also a specific reflection of the relations of production. When the agricultural productive forces are at a low level and restricted to single operations, the farmers can only produce the grain or half of the grain they need for their own use and they have no alternative employment,

CHAPTER II RURAL LAND SYSTEM REFORM

then small-scale household operation has great vitality. The peasants will give up their land only when the productive forces are well developed and the stage of stable non-agricultural production is reached. Second, the most important thing is economic benefits. Though the farmland belongs to the collective the peasants have gained the use right of the land through contracting it, so naturally they have the right to get the benefit from the land. That means that the farmers occupy part of the public resources. No matter what kind of changes may occur in the land use right and operation method, they will not give up the land use right easily. In some economically developed areas the allocation of resources and employment is done in a unified way by the local administrations, relying on the collective's great economic strength and advanced operational methods. When the land is used by the collective the farmers can get more stable incomes than by cultivating the farmland by themselves. In this way, the land is comparatively centralized and the operation scale is expanded. But in most areas this can not be done, as the land needs to be circulated and centralized. Therefore, we have to find the answer in the land system itself.

The present rural situation in China does not meet the requirements for land centralization and expanding of operation scale. But we know that during the reform of the past decade or so great changes have taken place in the rural economy and the society which have had a great impact on the land system.

Following the changes in the rural economic structure and operational mechanism, a demand for land circulation and the optimization of key elements has been put forward. Land is the basic element of agricultural production; only the establishment of an effective and flexible land circulation mechanism can realize the optimization of the relevant labor, funds and technology, and raise its utilization rate. The establishment of the land system includes defining and standardizing rights, and perfecting the operational methods and management system. The stress of the work has to be put on land circulation.

Land circulation is an inevitable outcome of rural economic and social development. So a flexible and effective land circulation system has to be established to meet the objective requirements of rural economic development.

First, changes in the rural industrial structure and employment structure inevitably lead to the demand for land circulation. At present, about 100 million rural laborers are working in non-agricultural economic sectors. However, they do not want to separate themselves from the land completely, because of the lack of a modern social insurance system. If a flexible and effective land circulation system is established in the countryside, they can transfer their land freely when they do not want to cultivate it and get it back when they want to return to farming. Only in this way, can the farmers' worries be dispelled.

In the countryside, while some farmers are working in non-agricultural economic sectors, others are taking the road of professional farming. They have become wealthy by developing high-efficiency agriculture with high output and fine-quality farm products. They are the pillars of agricultural production because they applied advanced techniques and management methods. At the same time, they have the conditions and also the desire to expand the production scale. At the present time they want more land. But when market demand shrinks or when they meet some difficulties in production they have to reduce their production scale. So they have to reduce their land area. The expansion and reduction of production scale and increase and reduction of land area cause the circulation and regrouping of various elements of production, which are the necessary factors for the development of the market economy, and also the inevitable outcome of the development of the market economy. In order to meet this objective requirement, a flexible land circulation mechanism has to be established.

Second, land circulation is the inevitable outcome of the changes in the members (labor force) and production ability of the farm households. The labor force changes frequently because of natural and social factors, such as birth, old age, sickness, death, marriage, members joining the army, being promoted, going away to school, going to work in factories, etc. The land area should be adjusted following the changes in manpower and production ability of the farm households. Therefore, the establishment of a flexible land circulation mechanism can make the households which have more manpower and better production ability but less land get more land easily, and the households which have less manpower and more land transfer their land easily. Only in this way can the combination of the land and other production elements gradually be rationalized and the agricultural productive forces properly used.

At the same time, we should point out that the land-use right may not only be circulated among the farmers within the collective, it may also be circulated among different economic entities, leaving aside the state use of rural collective land. There are two conditions for land circulation: The first one is circulation among different collectives caused by the proper concentration of township enterprises in a certain area and the construction of small towns. The second one is the land ownership circulation caused by unbalanced economic development. Some collectives with an earlier start and solid foundation for their development, have tended to expand their land to meet the needs of their developing productive forces. While hiring workers from other places and collecting funds by issuing stocks and bonds, they also gain land ownership or long-term land-use right through purchase or other methods.

In a word, following the development of rural industry, socialization of production and the gradual development of the rural market economy, an unbalanced development situation has tended to appear in the rural economy. So circulation and combinations of various elements of production between households, units and regions will be unavoidable. And land, a basic element of production, will surely be part of this process. Therefore, the establishment of a flexible and highly effective rural land circulation mechanism is the objective demand of rural economic development.

2. The search for the ideal land circulation system.

A series of studies have been made in the countryside on the problems of adjustment and division of land which have cropped up recently. How to define the property right of the land and how to stabilize the management right of the contracted land are the key issues. In some cases the land is divided up into pieces that are economically unfeasible. At the same time, farmers are reluctant to invest in their contracted land because of the frequent readjustment of the land. Two solutions have been tried: First, the contracted period may be extended and the land will not be readjusted or redivided because of an increase in the number of family members after the contracts are signed. The long-term contract relationship between the collective and the household should be clarified. In some places, village committees have been set up and they become the counterparts with which the farm household sign the contracts for the land. In some mountain areas the village cooperative economic organizations are considered the owners of the collective land. The hilly land is leased to the peasant households for a period of 70 years or more. A land-use permit is issued by the county people's governments or higher-level people's governments. During the contracted period the owner has the right to collect rents and the lessee has the right to transfer the land or raise a mortgage on it during the contract period. Second, the contract period will not be extended and new members of the households will have the right to receive their portions of the land. Any adjustment should be standardized through the establishment of the land system, and rent distribution may substitute for readjustment of the land.

The purpose of land circulation is to increase the flexibility of the elements of production and ensure effective arrangement of the resources. But practice has shown that not all instances of land circulation lead to a more efficient arrangement of the resources. On the contrary, land circulation often worsens the income distribution and retards the income increase because of the shortage of non-agricultural employment opportunities and population pressure. Only by increasing non-agricultural employment opportunities and reducing pressure on the land can land circulation improve the income distribution and increase incomes. At present, in some places where there has been a large-scale exodus from the land there is a great demand for land circulation. In order to handle this situation the following three forms of land circulation may be applicable: a. The land-use right can be transferred freely among the households approved by the relevant governments, bringing land circulation into the open and legalizing it; b. The land can be circulated by collective mandatory order. In some developed areas peasant households return the land to the collective or the land is taken back by compulsory measures and then the land is transferred to other households. Direct transfer is not allowed in these areas; c. The land can be transferred among the peasant households, but this has to be approved by village organizations and the applicants have to go through the relevant formalities. About 78 percent of the villages in Pingdu County, Shandong Province, have adopted this last method.

3. Lack of regulations and standards for land circulation.

Though an article covering land transfer was added in the amendments to the Constitution in 1988 and policies for land transfer were stipulated in a document issued by the central government in the late 1980s, there are still no legal documents specially stipulating the scale, procedure or management method as regards land transfer. Therefore, the transfer of agricultural land is conducted under the spontaneous guidance of local governments.

The imperfect systems of land ownership and land circulation make the land management system fragile; there is a lack of records and serious land disputes are the result.

4. The new changes in land management require the circulation of land-use rights.

Since the introduction of the household contract responsibility system, linking remuneration to output, the rural management system has been gradually perfected, the land system in the countryside has also been changing. It is adapting itself to the commercialization, socialization and modernization of agricultural production and revitalizing land management.

The changes in the methods of land management have shown that the concept of land being a kind of capital has been gradually formed. The land is no longer dominated by the planned economy, and its value increases day by day. Its scale of use and social function are increasingly expanding, and its use-right is circulated in various ways. Though there are still some problems in land circulation which should be solved promptly, there is an irresistible trend toward letting market forces control the use-right of land. Therefore, we should do more work to make land management suit China's situation and the needs of the market economy.

5. Farmers' interests should be protected in land circulation.

In studying farmland use, we should not forget the most basic prerequisite—the Constitution and laws stipulate that "land in the rural and suburban areas is owned by collectives, except for those portions which belong to the state in accordance with the law." And, "The use right of the land owned by the state and collectives may be transferred. No organization or individual may appropriate, buy, sell or lease land, or unlawfully transfer land in other ways." This means that the land owned by the collective belongs to the members of the collective and can not make free transfer to anyone or any organization outside the collective under any circumstances. The members of the collective have the right to gain profits from the collective land.

In recent years the collective and peasants' interests have often been infringed upon. Some places have practiced intensive farming in the countryside and they can not correctly handle the relationship between the contracted right of the peasants and the collective ownership of the land. So sometimes the contract system is undermined. In some places the use of the land by a collective enterprise is free of charge, and the use by an individual enterprise is also either free or very cheap. Sometimes land is sold for non-agricultural use outside the collective for a low price. The buyer can earn a lot of money from the land by doing real estate business. But the local farmers earn no profits from the sale. In some other places, the collectives use the money earned from selling land to engage in industry or sideline production. Or some accomplish nothing by wasting the money. As a result, the peasants lose their source of income—the land-use right—and the collectives lose control of their land. The collective land ownership and household contract system are actually harmed by such sales.

CHAPTER II RURAL LAND SYSTEM REFORM

(II) The Market Mechanism and Land Circulation

The establishment of market economy system in China means that the market mechanism will be the basic lever for the arrangement of resources. There is no substitute for land as the fundamental means of production. To realize land circulation through market mechanism is the historical and logical development of the market economy. Market regulation of land circulation has the following advantages: a. It is favorable for farmers to make their own decisions about land cultivation. Practice has proved that the irregular adjustment of the land destabilizes the land contract relationship, and the rights and interests of the farmers, as independent producers of commodities, can not be respected or protected. Only the establishment of a land circulation system on the basis of the market economy can allow the farmers to decide on the expansion or reduction of production scale in line with the market situation. b. Disproportions between land and laborers can be adjusted promptly, allowing the dynamic regrouping of the agricultural factors of production. c. The market regulation of land circulation includes compensated transfer and exchange at equal value. In this way, farmers' worries about investment in their land, especially long-term input, will be dispelled, and intensive farming favored. d. The compensational and competitive character of the market mechanism is conducive to the proper circulation and concentration of farmland. China has a large population but relatively little arable land, and so land is the treasure of the Chinese people. However, in some places the prices of agricultural products are too low, making farming unprofitable. Nevertheless, the farmers are reluctant to abandon their land-use rights, because they can transfer their land for payment. This promotes land concentration and large-scale farming, as the decision-making right about land adjustment is in the hands of the peasants. Thus frequent and arbitrary changes in land usage are avoided.

The rural land market is composed of two parts: the land ownership market and land use-right market.

The land ownership market includes the compensated transfer of land ownership between the collective and the state or between collectives. These transfers of land ownership do not infringe upon the public ownership of the land, but in fact raise the efficiency of the use of the land. Therefore, this kind of land market should be recognized and gradually improved.

The land use-right market is a land leasing market involving two kinds of leasing: First, the collective organizations transfer the land use-right to the members of the collective, other collective organizations or individuals (this is hereafter referred to as the first-class land market); second, the land users transfer their land to other people during the contract period. This land can be transferred again or several times (this is hereafter referred to as the second-class land market). The land use-right circulated among the land users belongs to the second-class market.

Meanwhile, the first-class land market will be an incomplete market for a period of time because of the nature of collective ownership of the land and the objective necessity of protecting the interests of the farmers. On the one hand, collective ownership means that the land has to be used equally by each member of the collective. If the land is transferred by competitive methods, such as public bidding, that means denying the rights of some collective members, because the majority of farmers cannot live without land. On the other hand, in order to protect the rights and interests of farm households the state must exercise strict control over the first-class land market.

As far as the second-class land market is concerned, the state land departments and the land owners should exercise supervision and control over the use of the land. The land areas, rent, methods of transfer, etc., should be freely negotiated by the persons concerned, so as to bring the market mechanism into full play.

The following three problems should be solved in order to standardize the land market:

1. Rural land property rights should be scientifically demarcated and a land system of collective ownership and cultivation by farm households should be perfected.

On the property right of land, there are two points which

CHAPTER II RURAL LAND SYSTEM REFORM

should be made clear: One, the owner of each plot of land —township, village or other organization—should be made clear, and land ownership certificates should be issued. Two, what kind of land rights belong to the collective and what kind belong to the farm households should be made clear, such as ownership, right of possession (contracting and operating), right to lease, right to buy and sell, right of inheritance, right of mortgage, usufruct, and right of planning or using for other purposes. The economic and legal status of the farmers as independent commodity producers should be established along with the development of the market economy. Farmers should be given more power to make their own decisions concerning the land; except for the right of planning, right of using for other purposes, final ownership and part of the usufruct, all other rights should be exercised by the farmers themselves. This is the same as giving all legal person property rights to enterprises during the reform of the system of state enterprises.

2. Standardized management of land registration is an important foundation for establishing and perfecting the land market.

We should accomplish the following tasks: First, an overall investigation of the quality, quantity, location and utilization of the land should be carried out; second, an economic evaluation of the land should be completed. Evaluation groups should be organized by land managers, specialists in the agricultural economy, rural cadres and farmers' representatives to grade and evaluate the land in accordance with the location, fertility of the soil, output value of the land and the experience of the teams; third, collective organizations and farm households should register their land at state land management departments in conformity with legal provisions, and land property right certificates should be issued; fourth, land references and records should be sorted out and taken good care of to provide useful data for the operation of the land market and rural land management.

3. A rural land circulation supervision system should be worked out and perfected to ensure the normal circulation of the land in the countryside.

Based on the situation in the countryside, appropriate and

practical regulations concerning rural land circulation management should be stipulated. The most important issues, such as the conditions of, and procedures and prices for land transfer, the responsibility for breaking a contract and regulation of profits should be standardized by law. Land circulation which accords with the demands of the development of the rural productive forces should be encouraged and guaranteed, and opportunistic actions which obstruct the development of the rural economy should be curbed. Only in this way can the operation of the rural land market be put on a healthy track.

(III) Appropriate Scale Management Leads to the Proper Arrangement of the Elements of Agricultural Production

The long-standing planned economic system has hampered the proper arrangement of the elements of production, causing low agricultural productivity and profits, and hindering self-development. The establishment of the market economic system provides favorable conditions for the rational arrangement of the elements of production, while scale management is the best form for realizing their proper arrangement.

The necessity for the development of scale management in agriculture may be summarized as follows:

1. The development of the rural reform requires appropriate scale management of agriculture.

There is no doubt that the responsibility system practiced in the early stage of the rural reform has played a positive role in arousing the enthusiasm of the peasants and in increasing production and incomes. But, following the deepening of the reform and changes in rural conditions some problems have cropped up. For example, the land is contracted out on average according to the number of people in the collective, and this has resulted in it being fragmented into small plots which are inconvenient for the mechanization of agriculture and scientific farming. Under the responsibility system more labor and costs are consumed in production than are necessary according to the principle of labor division and cooperation according to labor function. As a result, capable farmers who are willing to engage in farming do not have enough land, while others, who do not want to cultivate their small plots, let the land lie waste. In addition, in some areas, in order to cut down on expenses farm households have refused to accept social services, and some have even sold their tractors or other farm machines and bought oxen in order to farm their small plots of land more cheaply. And machine seeding has been abandoned in favor of hand spreading. These factors have restricted economic development and rural reform in the undeveloped rural areas.

2. Scale management is the practical choice.

Farming will still be the chief way for people to increase their incomes in the underdeveloped rural areas for quite a long period of time to come. The scale of agricultural management is an important factor deciding the speed of increase of the farmers' incomes. Surveys have shown that the ideal farming area is about two hectare per household under the present production conditions. If the scale of management is too small some of the labor force will be left unused and the development of mechanization will be restricted. At the same time, it is difficult to improve the administrative level, and the increase potential of the output is limited, so that fewer agricultural products will be sold on the market. As a result, the rate of increase of farmers' incomes will be slowed, while it will be difficult to shift the surplus rural labor to other fields of productivity. This is the reason for the slowing down of the urbanization of the countryside and sluggish development of nonagricultural economic pursuits.

3. Scale management for agriculture is of universal significance.

The key to scale management for agriculture is the proper arrangement of the production elements. This means that the production elements—land, labor, materials and techniques—should be matched well and given full play. First, using China's advantage of an abundant labor force, we should cultivate the land meticulously, develop more crops a year and substitute machine farming for manpower and livestock farming. Second, production conditions should be improved constantly, and advanced techniques, seeds, materials and farm machinery should be promoted. At the same time, the administrative level should be raised and production scale expanded. Third, seasonal shortages of production elements should be alleviated through better social services, cooperation among peasant households, renting of farm tools or farming by contractors.

The township governments (or collective village economic organizations) can rent out land which the relevant households do not wish to cultivate to agricultural enterprises or peasant households who are willing to enlarge their production scale. Practice has proved that this is a good way to develop scale management and transfer land with compensation.

Qiaoan Township, Tianchang County, Anhui Province was the first to adopt this method. The township government did a survey for the households who were engaged in nonagricultural economic sectors or whose farming results were poor. The survey took account of their input and output and the year's estimated economic results, as well as the average annual profit on their contracted land. Contracts were signed after negotiations between the related parties. The contents of the contracts included rent, contract period, and the rights and responsibilities of both parties. The townships (or villages) rent some or all of the land from these households temporarily or permanently.

The township governments first investigate the agricultural enterprises which are willing to rent out land and households specializing in farming. Then contracts are signed between the township governments and the qualified enterprises or households. Low-interest or interest-free loans are granted to those enterprises and households which have rented large areas of land for comparatively long periods and intend to invest a lot of money in the land.

In this situation it is inevitable that the phenomenon of re-renting should appear. Following the successful implementation of the household contract responsibility system in the first stage of rural reform farm households have become relatively independent commodity producers. But with the deepening of the rural reform the limitations of the contract system will become more apparent. The second stage of the rural reform will be

CHAPTER II RURAL LAND SYSTEM REFORM

completed following the resolving of the contradictions which have cropped up during the process of the reform. On this question, academic and theoretical circles have put forward many suggestions and opinions, such as developing the commodity economy, promoting industrialization in the countryside through the development of township enterprises, reforming the planned purchasing system and extending the management scale. Whatever the suggestions or opinions are they revolve around the millions of peasants and the land.

Re-renting is both possible and feasible. In some areas the grain output is high and the surplus manpower would rather leave their small pieces of land to find new jobs.

Most of these people are young and strong or have professional skills. They go to other counties or provinces to work in industry or do business with their families. Others work in township enterprises or the service sector in their hometowns.

The average annual per capita income is about 2,000 yuan in the above-mentioned households. The utilization ratio of their land and the grain output of these households are low; sometimes their land is left waste.

Most of the farmers who are still working on the land are experts at farming. They also engage in fish breeding and poultry raising and are keen to expand the area of their land.

These are the circumstances that make re-renting possible.

The practice of re-renting has alleviated, to a certain extent, the land shortage in some rural areas. So households specializing in grain growing can obtain more land and the households engaging in nonagricultural production can put their land to better use. In this way the land utilization ratio has been increased, per-unit area yield and total grain output have also increased, and more agricultural products are sold as commodities, thus consolidating, perfecting and developing the contracted household responsibility system, and developing and expanding scale management.

The land circulation has promoted the further division and transformation of labor power. The households which engage in nonagricultural production in the secondary and service industries can do so without worrying about their livelihood, even though they have left the land, and the households which work the land can extend their production scales and invest more in the land at their convenience. So each type of household complements the other.

But in the process of re-renting land, there are still many problems remaining to be solved. Some leaseholders who return to their hometowns want to take their land back. At the same time, some renters are still reluctant to enlarge their production scale and commit themselves to long-term investment for various reasons.

But re-renting is still considered an effective way for deepening the rural reform.

(IV) Scale Management Is a Long Historical Process. There Is no Contradiction Between the Large Market and Small-Scale Production, and Attention Should Be Paid to the Household Economy

1. Household management as a basic system should be stabilized over a long period of time.

The establishment of the household contract responsibility system in the course of rural reform has opened broad vistas for both the urban and rural household economies. Household management is compatible with the development of the present productive forces, and thus has great vitality. In the central and western areas of the country household management will be continuously practiced for quite a long period of time to come and will be the steady motive force for agricultural development. Scale management in this period means the development and enlargement of household management. Stabilizing household management is an essential aspect of the development of the rural economy and also the solid foundation for the appropriate development of scale management.

2. Scale management should be compatible with economic development in different phases, and imposing uniformity should be avoided.

Scale management will be a long historical process in China,

CHAPTER II RURAL LAND SYSTEM REFORM

going through the following phases:

The first is the traditional agriculture phase. In this period the input of elements of production mainly consists of land and manpower, because in this period self-supporting production occupies the dominant position. People are dependent on the land, which is also considered the guarantee of social welfare. At this time the whole of society begins to turn from being agricultural to being industrial. Not many alternative opportunities for employment are provided in this period, and the agricultural opportunity cost and marginal labor efficiency are very low. So at this time suitable agricultural organizations will be organized, represented by small-scale farming, mainly household operations. In this situation it is difficult and not economical to establish collective agriculture by forcibly amalgamating small-scale farming operations.

In the second phase industry has developed to a certain scale and the urban population has increased, thus promoting the rural division of labor and the development of commodity production. Under the guidance of the market, agricultural production will enter the market and agricultural products will be sold on the market. Though production is still managed by households, social services appear, in order to save exchange costs and increase service quality. Therefore, agricultural cooperative organizations and other commercial organizations spring up, providing various services for production.

As industry and urbanization develop further, farmers move from the rural to the urban areas, and at the same time labor wages and land and product prices increase. So the rural structure is basically changed. That is the third phase. Capital input into agriculture increases and land-intensive operations are turned into land- and manpower-economizing operations. The land, as the object of the input of capital, is pressured to concentrate. Grain production demands greater land concentration than other crops. Therefore, scale management is turned into a production link from being a service link. In turn, new demands are placed on services and there is pressure for a clearer division of labor.

3. The household is considered an organizational form of

social life. The existence and development of the household are on the basis of the development of the household economy. So great attention should be paid to household economy research and development.

There are two different viewpoints on the household economy. First, some people think that great attention should be paid to the development of the household economy. Each family is considered a cell of society. So the life of each family should be improved constantly in order that its members can live happy lives. The quality of family members should be improved too. This is the foundation for long-term peace and prosperity for the state. Others think that the state will wither away, and so the family will also die out. Therefore, they always hold negative attitude toward the household economy and related small-scale production. Each household functions in many ways, such as by multiplying its members, producing, accumulating and developing economically. It has a stake in education, health care, social and security, etc. In order to support the family, the household economy has to be developed so as to increase its income and improve the family members' standard of living and personal qualities.

The main characteristics of the household economy are as follows:

(1) It has great vitality. The household economy can adapt to any social circumstances, not only favorable conditions, but also adverse ones, and change its activities following changes in the modes of production.

(2) It has an independent character. Though the household economy is a small production unit it is autonomous when it comes to production, exchange, arrangement and consumption. It is self-sufficient by nature.

(3) It is capable of diversification. The household can develop its small-scale and simple reproduction mode or specialize in one product. They can also choose to engage in secondary or tertiary industry. Households are involved in fish breeding, poultry raising and processing, as well as commodity, cultural, educational and technical exchanges.

CHAPTER II RURAL LAND SYSTEM REFORM

China initiated its reform in the countryside and then spread it to the urban areas. The establishment of the household contract responsibility system was the most important step in the rural reform and has ushered in a new situation for the development of China's household economy.

In the course of carrying out the household responsibility system the household becomes a basic economic unit. The ownership of the land still belongs to the collective, but its use right belongs to the contracted households. In this way, the peasants are not only workers, as in the past, but also managers of the land. Thus, the enthusiasm of the farm households is brought into full play.

In addition, all the harvest belongs to the households, except for state purchase quotas and the portion which must be delivered to the collective, as stated in the contracts. This gives these households surplus grain and funds, providing them with the means to develop further.

The household responsibility system is beneficial to the proper arrangement of the elements of production. In the busy season all the family members can help the able-bodied farm workers bring in the harvest, while in the slack seasons they can engage in household sideline production, thus giving full play to the role of the family members.

In a word, the implementation of the household contract responsibility system has not only created a favorable situation for the development of the household economy but also brought vitality to the development of China's rural economy.

The rural household economy is the point of growth which propels the development of the rural economy; it is also a part of the commodity and market economies. The rural household economy is established on the basis of the public ownership of the means of production. The egalitarian distribution method has been abandoned and the principle of distribution according to work adopted. Different from the past natural economy, a new type of household economy under socialist conditions has emerged.

Owing to the increase of accumulation by farm households,

THE REFORM AND DEVELOPMENT OF CHINA'S RURAL ECONOMY

it has become possible for factories and other enterprises to be run by one household or by several households together in the countryside. In order to expand production, some household factories combine when they have developed to a certain level. This forms a new type of cooperative economy and also becomes the base for the development of the township economy. It represents a new level of development of the rural forces of production forces. At the same time, collectives, such as townships and towns, also run some key enterprises, involving thousands of families. Some towns and townships have established group companies to develop the regional economy. Geared to the market, some villages and townships produce one product or several products in batches. A large number of shops, hotels and restaurants have been built by individuals, farm households and others in the countryside. In addition, various associations, markets for farm produce and other kinds of markets have sprung up all over the country. At present, the rural economy is unprecedentedly prosperous and farm households are the mainstays of the rural markets.

Rural reform has in turn promoted urban reform. In cities there are also a lot of individuals and specialized households engaging in industry, and in the service trades, such as business, hotels, catering and information. Some households or groups of households even run factories and other types of business companies, or contract, rent or buy small state shops, factories and enterprises.

Tremendous changes have taken place in China's agriculture since the reform initiated by the Third Plenary Session of the 11th National Congress of the CPC. The rural economy has been revitalized and the living standards of farm households have been improved. But when there is fluctuation in agricultural production, especially in grain production, some people put the blame on the small-scale household management system. They think that it is the result of a contradiction between "big market and small-scale production," and suggest expanding the production scale.

In fact, small-scale production is not absolutely antagonistic

CHAPTER II RURAL LAND SYSTEM REFORM

to large-scale production, as it forms naturally following the development of production. The command system does not necessarily lead to the enlargement of production scale; big does not necessarily mean good. In industry, not all the factories are big. There are large-scale factories, medium- and small-scale ones and even household factories. Shops and stores also come in various sizes. However, the problem is how to realize appropriate scale management. Is it possible to concentrate the land and the labor force as in the past and to still practice egalitarianism? The answer is that the rural population will absolutely not accept it. We should know that scale management is a product of the natural development of the economy, and it can be realized only if the necessary conditions are provided. The most important condition is that the majority of the rural labor force should be transferred to other industries, and only a small part retained for farm work. And then farm work should be mechanized. This is, of course, not easy; it takes a great amount of money and material input. On the one hand, township enterprises have to be established to absorb the surplus rural labor force, which involves a great deal of investment. On the other hand, agricultural mechanization also needs a great amount of money to buy machinery. At present, China's developed coastal areas may start to practice scale management on a gradual basis because they are economically strong. But the central and western areas, especially the poor areas, do not yet have the conditions for this.

At present, it is difficult for China to practice scale management of land because the average per capita arable area is too small—and would be even if nine out of ten rural laborers transferred to other occupations. The most pressing task is to stop the further redistribution of land when the number of family members changes, such as when children are born or daughters-in-law added. In some places, the area of land per household contract is fixed, despite any increases in the number of members of the household. It is desirable that this practice be popularized in the rural areas.

III. Land Shares as a Form of Cooperative Economy

(I) The Practice of Land Shares Is the Core and Practical Choice for the Deepening of the Reform of the Land System and Is Conducive to Solving a Series of Related Problems

First, farm households are encouraged to buy shares in their own land using their right to participate in various cooperative organizations, agricultural development projects and scale management. They will receive profits regularly in accordance with their capital stock.

Second, the active social security function of land will be brought into play. The household contract responsibility system makes the land "life insurance" for the farmers. The practice of the land share system will ensure regular incomes for the farmers even when they are unable to work the land.

Third, the operation of the land share system is conducive to land circulation and concentration, and the transfer of surplus labor. As mentioned above, some farmers are working in township enterprises and others are working in the cities.

The aim of agricultural modernization is to change the situation of small-scale and scattered management, and to practice appropriate-scale management. Specialized division of labor, intensive farming and socialized services will be practiced so as to increase labor productivity and farmland output. As a result, farmers' incomes will be increased and more energy will be put into agricultural production. So the peasants can work at other occupations or in other places without any worries. At the same time, peasants who have long-term land-use rights can take out mortgages on their land to raise loans, which they can then invest in farming.

Joint-stock agricultural cooperative enterprises may be established. Households can buy shares in their land which are distributed according to the number of family members; at the end of the year grain ration and surplus products (net profit) will be

CHAPTER II RURAL LAND SYSTEM REFORM

distributed according to the value of the shares. The employees of agricultural enterprises may or may not be land share holders. The land share holders can ask for grain rations (basic standard) and extra dividends on the strength of the share certificates, which prove the transfer of land-use rights to cooperative enterprises. So the land-use rights can be circulated according to market principles and scale land management can be practiced in the process of practical economic operation. As a result, the output of the land and agricultural efficiency will be raised.

The land share system allows the farmers to obtain profits from land which is used for nonagricultural production, thus increasing their incomes.

Therefore, we can say that the land share system is the proper way to pursue rural reform in the present situation.

Not only the peasants' income will increase but gaps between the cities and countryside will be narrowed.

(II) Realizing the Overall Transformation of Rural Property Rights on the Basis of New Ideas on Land Property Rights

1. Township enterprises should be developed into stock enterprises or stock cooperative enterprises with clear property relations and more efficient mechanism.

Unclear property relations have restrained the further development of the township enterprises. Superficially, the property of the township enterprises belongs to all the members of their communities. But in fact the problem of unclear property relations also exists in township enterprises, just as in state-owned enterprises. They are administered by local governments, and so the development of the enterprises is restricted by administrative interference.

The key to solving this problem is to introduce joint-stock or cooperative share management. The farmers are allowed to buy shares on the basis of their land holdings, funds, techniques and labor so as to reorganize the property system of the township enterprises. In this way an internal motive force for the further development of the township enterprises will be produced.

Part or all the existing collective property can be divided into different shares for the relevant households, and the extra dividends can be distributed in the form of shares. A distribution system combining work and property should be established. In addition, the existing enterprises can be enlarged and new enterprises established by absorbing more shares from legal persons and foreign investment so as to promote the development of township enterprises and increase the farmers' income.

2. The intermediate rural service organizations should be standardized on the basis of the property relations of cooperative share management.

The development of intermediate rural service organizations run by local people should be energetically supported, as they are of great significance for the deepening of the rural reform. On the one hand, such organizations run by the local people provide services for the households or household enterprises. This is not only conducive to the consolidation of the household responsibility system but also makes it adaptable to the continuous development of marketization and socialization of the rural economy. On the other hand, the intermediate rural service organizations not only involve rural economic management but also rural social management. So the establishment and development of these intermediate organizations will directly affect the rural reform.

The scale and function of a household can not be compared with those of the intermediate rural service organizations run by the local people. The multi-service social function can only be performed by the intermediate organizations. For example, cooperatives are one form of such organizations. Farmers can become members of the cooperatives by buying shares and benefiting from social services in the links of production and circulation. The money paid for shares is used as a fund for the operation of the cooperatives, and their members can receive dividends every year. This kind of property relationship is not the same as that of stock companies and also different from that of the cooperatives in the past. It is full of vitality because it is closely connected with the farmers' interests.

3. The practice of the share system in credit cooperatives should be speeded up so as to realize the transformation of the

property right of the rural cooperative financial system.

At present, the credit cooperatives are independent accounting units assuming responsibility for their own profits and losses only in name. They are cooperative financial organizations under collective ownership, and at the same time they are basic departments of the Agricultural Bank, entrusted by the People's Bank of China. Large amounts of loans will be granted by the credit cooperatives, in line with state policy. In fact, the Agricultural Bank often uses the capital of the credit cooperatives to make up for insufficiencies in its own funds. Therefore, there is no way to ensure the independent operation of the credit cooperatives. The capital property right is not clear, and the proportion of shares owned by farmers in the credit cooperatives is low because of the continuous changes in their management, sometimes launched by the people and sometimes by the state. The most pressing task is to change the credit cooperatives into cooperative commercial and financial organizations of the farmers by unhooking their connections to the policy function of the state by selling shares. Their property right can be reorganized by selling stock right.

(III) Operating the Cooperative Share Economy in the Countryside, Focusing on the Land

The hazy concept of land property right means that the relationship between land ownership, land-contracting right and land-use right is not clear. When a farmer contracts a piece of land he thinks that the land ownership belongs to him, not clearly understanding the difference between the contracting right and ownership. This is a universal problem in the countryside. The property right should be further standardized through a land share cooperation system. To realize rural modernization, the land should be arranged and used in an overall and unified way. So new problems have appeared in the process of the implementation of the household responsibility system. The experiments in land reform performed by Nanhai, Guangdong Province, show that a new rural land property right system should be worked out in order to solve this new contradiction.

The basic principle for the establishment of a new land

property right system is to insist on continuing the rural cooperative economy. The forms of the collective economic organization and its property should be maintained and the malpractice of excessive consolidation should be get rid of in the new land property system. The land property right could be divided into ownership and land legal person property right. The ownership should be ultimately returned to the peasants and the land share property right should belong to the joint-stock cooperative economic organization.

The reform of the rural land property right system means practicing a land share cooperation system. The land may be distributed to the farmers by means of different shares according to age groups. The converted price could be fixed at the purchasing price for land stipulated by the state, or depending on their economic efficiency. This system would separate the value of land ownership and the use value of the legal person property right of an enterprise, and would assist the overall planning and rational use of the land. The land can be divided into farmland protection area, industrial development area and business and accommodation area. In this way, the contradiction between rural modernization and land property right could be solved properly. It would be another breakthrough in rural reform to substitute the land share cooperation system for the traditional collective economy following the implementation of the household contract responsibility system. Under the household contract responsibility system the land still belongs to the collective, and the peasants only have the right to use the land. The land property right of the collective economy has not been changed. However, the land share cooperation system discards the traditional land property right of the collective economy.

The land share cooperation system will promote the implementation of the rural share cooperation system. Property assessment will be carried out on the collective tertiary and industrial sectors, and then the total value of the property will be converted into shares to be distributed to each person. Share certificates will be issued. Withdrawal of shares will not be allowed, so as to maintain the nature of the rural cooperative economy with

Chinese characteristics and stabilize the cooperative economy. The income of the share-issuing cooperative economic organizations will be distributed in the form of shares after deductions for taxes and public welfare and accumulation funds.

(IV) The Share Cooperation System—A System with Vitality

The share and cooperative systems have a long history, during which they have been used in various forms by commercial production managers. Valuable experience has been gained, and by practicing the share cooperation system the farmers will be able to establish modern enterprises, another step toward the establishment of a modern enterprise system nationwide.

The share and cooperation systems are basic systems directly dealing with the combination and circulation of resources in market economy conditions. These systems are mainly microeconomic, no matter the nature of the enterprises. Therefore, the share system can be used in various trades. At present, the share cooperation system, an effective way to realize modernization, is not only being adopted by enterprises in the countryside, but also by units involved in farming, forestry, animal husbandry, fisheries, development of land resources and the service trades.

The share cooperation system separates the formation of material objects and form of value of the property. So the property can be concentrated to optimize the productive forces. The concentration and circulation of property in the form of value will promote the formation of economies of scale for the elements of production and the optimization of resources. At the same time, the property right becomes clear in the form of value. So a standardized system for ownership and management right (controlling right) will be established. An effective method has been found for the collective economy in China's countryside to improve its property right system. At present, collective property is being converted into shares and distributed to individuals. Land in the countryside is also being converted into shares and cultivated cooperatively. The same is true in the forest regions.

Under the share cooperation system the various production elements, such as capital, land, factory buildings, equipment, labor forces and intellectual property rights, can be used to buy shares in the enterprises which are managed by the people according to their shareholdings, and the profits and risks are also divided according to their shareholdings. The responsibilities and rights of the owners, managers and workers should be clarified so as to increase the efficiency of the enterprises. In this way, enthusiasm for taking part in economic activities by the owners of the elements of production will be brought into full play.

The share cooperation system will display its effectiveness in both the production and operating mechanisms. Its most outstanding effect on the production mechanism will be in getting rid of the traditional closed nature of the household, family ties, community, region and industry, and urban and rural exclusiveness by promoting the opening up to the outside. In line with the practical developments of specialization and socialization, and the requirements of the market, enterprises may be established jointly through the bringing together of various elements of production. Its effect on the operating mechanism will be to give an impetus to the development of the enterprises and bring the enthusiasm of people of various levels into full play. Moreover, it can have the effect of freeing enterprises from unwarranted outside interference and allowing them to be independent in management. Corresponding and effective labor, accumulation, management and risk-bearing systems can be established through the defining of the rights and interests of the workers and staff members, who will have a material interest in the progress of their enterprises.

The share cooperation system can effectively solve the pressing problems of enlarging management scale and establishing a stable enterprise system and provide the optimum mode for the development of the rural structure characterized by a variety of economic elements.

Chapter III
The Marketization of the Purchase and Sales Systems of Agricultural Products

I. Pushing Forward the Reform of the Purchase and Sales Systems with Marketization as the Objective

(I) We Should Correctly Estimate the Supply and Demand Situation of Agricultural Products in the Near Future, and not Be Pessimistic

Agriculture, the farmers and the rural economy have become some the most important issues attracting the concern of the whole of society. Of special concern are the questions of whether the market supply of and demand for agricultural and sideline products can be stabilized or not, and if the rise of food prices can be effectively restrained. But we should refrain from overestimating the seriousness of the situation for the following four reasons:

First, there is no big problem in terms of the supply of and demand for agricultural and sideline products produced and consumed by farmers themselves. Peasants even in backward regions have enough to eat, and in fact eat better than ever before. Only peasants in disaster-ridden and poverty-stricken areas have difficulty getting enough to eat, a fact which is not a threat to China's economic situation as a whole. Over 80 percent of the Chinese people have a reliable food supply.

Second, as to agricultural and sideline products produced by peasants and consumed by residents of small cities and towns, the balance between supply and demand is not a serious problem.

With small-radius markets, price mechanisms can regulate not only production, but also consumption. So the gap between supply and demand can easily be filled.

Third, among agricultural and sideline products consumed by residents of large and medium-sized cities, both the supply of and demand for high- and medium-grade foodstuffs with a high degree of marketization and price elasticity are vigorous, and there is no trace of any crisis. Even if there is a shortage of supply and prices increase while consumption declines, nevertheless, a balance will soon be restored.

Fourth, in large and medium-sized cities the foodstuffs for which a balance between supply and demand is difficult to achieve are those consumed by low-income people. A balance is also difficult to achieve in the case of the raw materials consumed by state-owned light industrial enterprises. This is because no matter how prices change there is little change in the level of consumption. Nevertheless, we should not overestimate the severity of the supply and demand situation for these agricultural and sideline products. Because: a. The current slight shortage of agricultural products is not chronic. A few years ago, peasants had difficulty selling grain. b. The rate of price rises for agricultural products is not higher than that of the prices of industrial products and is not higher, in particular, than that of the prices for means of production for agricultural use. This indicates that China's agricultural sector, including grain and cotton, which have supply and demand difficulties, is not the basic stimulator of price rises.

In the past couple of years the alarming instability in the supply of and demand for agricultural products has been apparent only in foodstuffs which people with low incomes in large and medium-sized cities consume, as well as in some agricultural raw materials necessary for enterprises with low efficiency to maintain their operations. Therefore, the supply and demand crisis in agricultural products in the past one or two years is a partial and periodic phenomenon rather than an all-round agricultural crisis that affects the whole economic situation. The essence of the problem is that the effective demand from some residents and

CHAPTER III MARKETIZATION OF PURCHASE AND SALES SYSTEMS

enterprises in cities for basic agricultural products is insufficient, i.e., they can not purchase agricultural products at the market prices.

At present, almost all agricultural countermeasures focus on how to increase the effective supply of agricultural products. If the current crux of the problem—insufficient effective demand for some products—is ignored, the supply of basic agricultural products such as grain and cotton will not be effectively stimulated.

The real difficulties for quite a long period to come are: On the one hand, it is impossible to rapidly increase the effective demand for grain, cotton and other primary agricultural products because the low-income population in large and medium-sized cities and the number of enterprises which constantly lack raw materials will decrease rather than increase within a short period of time. On the other hand, the country's grain-sown areas have not increased remarkably, the prices of chemical fertilizers have gone up and the gap between supply and demand is large.

In these circumstances, special attention should be paid to farmers' psychology; if farmers hold onto their grain, waiting for the right price at which to sell but misjudge the market, it will undoubtedly make the problem worse.

To stabilize the market supply of and demand for agricultural products in the current situation, experts have proposed the basic countermeasures of analyzing the problem, assigning responsibilities, unifying restraints and carrying out a variety of experiments, in addition to reinforcing the dynamics of the reform.

Analyzing the Problem The real sufferers in the current supply-demand crunch are urban people with low incomes and enterprises with poor economic returns. Therefore, it should be made clear that today the government is not able to, and should not, offer food subsidies to all urban citizens. Instead, it can only concentrate its limited financial resources on ensuring that the people with the lowest incomes have enough to eat and wear. When this principle is adhered to, the severity of the problem will be reduced by 50 percent. The other 50 percent is a technical problem as to how to distinguish the people with low incomes from all residents.

Assigning Responsibilities The responsibility for solving the problem of the food supply for low-income urbanites and the supply of agricultural raw materials for certain enterprises should not be all placed on the central government, but be mostly left to local authorities to shoulder.

Unifying Restraints Experience has shown that letting each province or autonomous region take all responsibility for agriculture easily leads to orders being issued and the operation of the market forces being hampered, thus forming man-made obstructions to the streamlining of supply and demand. Therefore, provincial control must be tempered by unified national restraints. The most important step at present is to prohibit barriers to the circulation of grain and other agricultural products being erected among regions. Also to be prohibited is the compulsory purchase of grain at low prices. If these two restraints are put in place no big problems will appear in the countryside.

Carrying Out a Variety of Experiments Localities may adopt various methods to solve the problem of stabilizing the agricultural supply and demand situation under unified restraints.

Meanwhile, the reform of state-owned enterprises in the following three sectors should be quickened: First, state-owned enterprises which take agricultural products as raw materials, generate low economic returns and suffer chronic losses may be allowed to go bankrupt or be reorganized to ensure the supply of agricultural raw materials to those with high economic returns. Second, the reform dynamics of the enterprises producing means of production for agricultural use should be reinforced so as to increase their economic returns, reduce costs, strengthen management and curb price rises for means of production for agricultural use. Third, the reform of the state-owned grain and food management sectors should be speeded up. We should break away from the monopoly position of the "main channels" and ensure competitive management with a variety of channels and cultivate intermediate organizations integrating the farmers with the market.

CHAPTER III MARKETIZATION OF PURCHASE AND SALES SYSTEMS

(II) Pushing Forward the Reform of the Purchase and Marketing System of Agricultural Products Under the Pressure of Inflation

China has carried out reforms of the purchase and marketing system of agricultural products several times. The latest reform started at the beginning of 1993, when most regions of the country abolished the system of buying grain by contract, and most cities and towns also abolished the supply of grain at state-set prices and lifted all controls from grain purchase and sale prices. In the same year the central rural work meeting put forward guidelines as follows: The fixed quotas for the purchase of grain should remain unchanged, while grain prices should be allowed to fluctuate in light of market conditions. However, at the end of 1993, when grain prices went up by a large margin, the state continued to set unified grain prices and purchase grain by contract. In addition, the central government clearly required grain departments to purchase 80 billion *jin* (1 *jin* = 0.5 kg) of grain at negotiated prices as well as purchasing 100 billion *jin* of grain according to contracts, so as to control grain resources. After the autumn of 1994 the prices of grain, cotton and other basic agricultural products went up by a large margin once again, which was the major factor in inflation in that year. In this situation, the central government had to require state-owned grain departments to hang out price signs while selling rationed grain and forbade grain merchants and grain-using units to purchase grain directly from the countryside but only at grain wholesale markets above the county level. In line with this policy, some towns and cities restored the grain rationing system. Some places even closed down grain markets and restricted the sales of grain to certain locations. Consequently, the reform of the grain purchase and marketing system in some places took a step backward rather than going forward.

The reform of the purchase and marketing system of agricultural products oscillated along with the fluctuations in the supply of and demand for agricultural products, raising some intriguing questions.

First, how can one estimate the prospects for the long- and medium-term balance between the supply of and demand for cotton, grain and other basic agricultural products? Different estimations of the prospects will give rise to different views. By reference to past experience, it is easy to be pessimistic when the supply of agricultural products runs short and their prices shoot up sharply. As a result, many people will not believe that the market mechanism can harmonize supply and demand in this sphere, which will affect the adoption of policies. On the other hand, if China is rich in agricultural products an optimistic estimation may be widely accepted.

Second, how can we analyze the relations between inflation and the reform of the purchase and marketing system for agricultural products during the transition from the planned economy to the market economy? The rise of food prices in the large and medium-sized cities played the main role in the rise of the consumer price index, making up about 60 percent. This phenomenon has given rise to two opposite judgments. One holds that this round of inflation in China was touched off by rises in the prices of agricultural products. To prevent overall malignant inflation, China must restrain such price rises, even, if necessary, promoting large-scale agricultural operations by amalgamating farm household management to spur production. The opposite judgment is that the current inflation is system-related, i.e., the government has issued too much money. The system-related inflation can only be fundamentally restrained by speeding up the reform of the state-owned sector. To control the prices of agricultural products by administrative means can only disturb the balance between supply and demand and will do harm to rather than help the macroeconomic balance.

Third, is it possible to continually push forward the reform of the purchase and marketing system of agricultural products in conditions of inflation? Not long ago, the State Council decided that the basic policy on the purchase and marketing of grain, cotton and chemical fertilizer should be decided by the provincial governor or municipal mayor. However, different from the former method—the central government controlling grain resources in

CHAPTER III MARKETIZATION OF PURCHASE AND SALES SYSTEMS

a unified way through state-owned grain operations—the new system is a big step forward, i.e., each province or municipality directly under the central authorities may balance supply and demand in the sectors of foodstuffs and industrial raw materials through provincial markets, other provinces' markets and international markets. In other words, the central government requires each province (or centrally administrated municipality) to realize a balance between supply and demand in the case of primary agricultural products. As to the means of achieving this balance, no rigid uniformity should be sought, but more recourse should be made of the market mechanism.

(III) Reforming and Perfecting the Means of Macro Control While Speeding Up the Marketization of the Prices of Agricultural Products

1. The problems that confront macro control in the course of marketization.

The sharp fluctuations in the prices of agricultural products and the changeable policies concerning prices fully indicate that the government's macro control can not be adapted to the requirements of the marketization of agricultural product prices. However, lifting controls from grain prices is the key to the marketization of agricultural products. After the autumn of 1993, when grain prices began to rise, the government immediately intervened by proclaiming administrative measures. But the farmers were very dissatisfied. This indicates that how the government can adapt itself to the trend of marketization of the prices for agricultural products and carry out correct and effective macro control means is still a big problem. In light of the current situation, the main jobs needing to be tackled are as follows:

First, changing the situation which the government controls the supply of some important means of agricultural production by administrative means. The quantity of supply of means of agricultural production and their price levels have greatly increased the production costs of agricultural products, and directly led to the fluctuation of the prices for agricultural products by a large margin. Take chemical fertilizers as an example. Between

October 1992 and March 1993 the prices of chemical fertilizers more than doubled after several price readjustments. Though the government set maximum prices, real prices continued to rise after March 1993, thus turning the highest set prices into the lowest protection prices. Meanwhile, more than two million tons of chemical fertilizer imported from abroad did not arrive on time in 1993. Consequently, the quantity of production goods for agricultural use declined while their prices went up, inevitably leading to the rise of prices for agricultural products. This is a reflection of the impact of the law of value on agricultural product prices, as a consequence of their marketization.

Second, government purchase of a certain proportion of grain, cotton and other major agricultural products by compulsory means must be abolished, as it runs counter to the market regulation mechanism.

In early 1993, after the control over grain prices was lifted all over the country, most places allowed prices to fluctuate along with market changes, while the fixed quotas for purchasing grain remained unchanged. Meanwhile, the government declared the adoption of the lowest protection prices set at the original level of purchasing prices. Due to government intervention in the marketization of agricultural products, the actual prices of such products were much lower than their proper prices. Consequently, on the one hand, farmers' enthusiasm for growing grain greatly declined, resulting in an imbalance between supply and demand. On the other hand, the formally restrained prices of some agricultural products would rise sharply whenever there was an opportunity in the limited market for agricultural products for them to seek their real value. This is what caused the great fluctuations in prices for grains and other agricultural products between 1993 and 1994.

Third, we must change the way the government regulates the relations between agricultural products' supply and demand through the state-owned business sector. This is because this system does not suit the requirements of the marketization of agricultural products and stimulates the fluctuation of agricultural products' prices.

CHAPTER III MARKETIZATION OF PURCHASE AND SALES SYSTEMS

After the implementation of the marketization of agricultural product prices, the state should set up stockpiles of the major products and regulate their prices so as to control the markets for agricultural products and dampen fluctuations in their prices.

One of the important causes for the sharp fluctuation of agricultural product prices after October 1993 was that state-owned grain enterprises did not purchase grain at the state protection prices, with an eye to increasing their profits, making a fiasco of the state's attempt to control grain markets through policies. Meanwhile they monopolized the markets in order to raise prices.

2. While establishing the rural market economy, China should reform the macro management system and perfect the means of macro control with speeding up the marketization of agricultural products' prices as the objective.

The repeated sharp fluctuations in agricultural product prices in the past two years indicate that in the course of promoting the rural market economy China's macrocontrol system was seriously backward and unsuited to the market economy, and the means of macro regulation and control were quite immature. Hence China must speed up the reform of its macromanagement system and greatly improve its methods of macro control.

The government should stop monopolizing the means of agricultural production. It should lift controls from the supply and prices of means of production and institute a competitive business system to guarantee sufficient supply of the means of agricultural production, with stable prices. a. The enterprises dealing in means of agricultural production should separate the functions of the government from those of enterprises, run businesses on their own and face the market competition. b. Investment in the production of means of agricultural production by various forms of ownership, such as joint ventures and exclusive foreign investment, should be encouraged so as to increase production, guarantee the supply of the means of agricultural production and improve the relations between supply and demand. c. The monopolized operation of the means of agricultural production should be abolished, and competitive operations should be implemented. Meanwhile, the systems of planned supply and government-set prices should be abolished and prices should be formed by the market. d. The government may regulate and control the supplies and price levels of the means of agricultural production through economic and legal means, such as the adoption of necessary maximum prices, financial subsidies, exemption from and reduction of taxes, preferential loans and increased imports.

China should thoroughly transform the purchase and marketing system of agricultural products, and adopt flexible operations to ensure that agricultural products enter the market directly. a. State-planned purchase by order or by contract should be done away with, together with all controls on the production and operation of agricultural products, to guarantee the effective formation of markets for agricultural products. b. State-fixed prices should also be abolished to guarantee that agricultural product prices are set by the market. c. A special storage system for major agricultural products should be set up, and the items to be stored should be purchased by the government at the current market prices. d. The situation in which state-owned business sectors monopolize the markets for agricultural products should be rectified, and multi-element, multi-form and multi-channel circulation should be encouraged. In this regard, farmers should be urged to directly enter circulation in an organized way and engage in competitive operations.

China should set up and perfect a state policy-related regulation and control system, and completely separate policy-related business from operation-related business. a. The state's main storage regulation system of main agricultural products should be separated from existing operations dealing with agricultural products. A storage regulation system directly under the State Council to regulate and control the national agricultural products market in a unified way should be set up. b. Risk funds should be established to deal with the shortage of major agricultural products resulting from natural disasters, wars and other major disasters. c. China should establish as soon as possible national unified

CHAPTER III MARKETIZATION OF PURCHASE AND SALES SYSTEMS

markets for agricultural products, eliminate regional and local circulation barriers, change the system of planned regional allocation of major agricultural products into autonomous market regulation. Efforts should be made to ensure that the different regions complement each other in terms of their agricultural advantages, regulating surpluses and maintaining a regional balance, thus laying the foundation for a national unified market regulated and controlled by macro policies.

In regulating and controlling agricultural product markets, the government should abandon the traditional administrative methods and make sure that these methods are not duplicated in the new systems and policies. a. The relative fluctuation of market prices for agricultural products is a normal phenomenon in market economies, being simply a reflection of the law of supply and demand. According to the experiences of advanced countries, it is a great success if grain market prices fluctuate between 15 and 20 percent. Therefore, we should not panic and resort to administrative measures at the first sign of fluctuation in the market. b. However, when the fluctuation exceeds a certain range or a warning line, we should adopt cautious measures to regulate and control it, eschewing compulsory means. c. In the past we used to resort to such measures as closing down the market, setting maximum prices, fixing the prices by state fiat, purchasing according compulsory plans, rationing in urban areas. All these methods run counter to the law of supply and demand and market regulation mechanisms. Such methods are obstacles to the marketization of agricultural products. d. We should be mindful of the fact that any return to a macrocontrol system featuring unstable policies will increase the cost of setting up a rural market economy.

3. In the course of promoting the marketization of agricultural product prices China should set up a corresponding rural macroeconomic control system.

The country should utilize financial policies to increase the input into agricultural infrastructure and strengthen the policy-related regulation of the agricultural products market. a. Increasing production and guaranteeing the balance between supply and demand are fundamental measures for stabilizing the agricultural products market. b. Another important step is to establish an agricultural products storage and regulation fund and agricultural products risk fund. The purpose of the former is to regulate the circulation of major agricultural products and stabilize the market, and of the latter, to alleviate the effects of natural disasters, wars and other unexpected occurrences. c. In coordination with policies concerning prices, industry and foreign trade, special subsidies may be offered to protect agriculture and stabilize prices. In addition, preferential treatment may be extended to some industries to encourage exports.

China should make use of tax policies to better protect agriculture and farmers' incomes and reduce the financial burden on rural people. a. In recent years the farmers have had to pay agricultural taxes and other charges, amounting up to 20 percent more of their incomes. The country should reform the agricultural taxation system and get rid of all the unreasonable charges. In this way, the farmers will only pay taxes. b. While setting the agricultural tax rate, the government should take into consideration how best to encourage backward agricultural sectors in the market economy and protect farmers' incomes. Tax rate should not be set too high or increase too fast. Agricultural tax should appropriately be reduced if necessary. Taxes imposed on township enterprises should be reduced so as to provide a flexible environment for the development of township enterprises.

China should perfect the rural financial regulation and control system, and guarantee the input of agricultural credits by means of financial policy-related regulation and control. a. We should set up and perfect as soon as possible the rural three-in-one financial system, and form a clear-cut division of work among policy-related banks, commercial banks and cooperative financial organizations so that they can coordinate closely with the rural financial system, guarantee agricultural credits, enliven and solidify rural financial operations. b. We should spare no effort to develop the rural financial market, and regulate the distribution and rational disposition of rural

CHAPTER III MARKETIZATION OF PURCHASE AND SALES SYSTEMS

resources, such as rural capital, technology and labor. c. After the reorganization of the rural financial system, agricultural banks and rural cooperative banks should operate completely according to commercial norms. Their loans will favor the regions and industries which have high economic returns, thus making it possible to further intensify the "de-agriculturalization" of rural capital. Hence the state should specify the scale and proportions of agricultural loans issued by rural commercial banks and should subsidize interest differences. Meanwhile, the government should include a certain proportion of capital in the annual currency issuing plan as special loans to rural cooperative banks so that they can issue rural production loans. Investment by the rural financial sector in agriculture should enjoy low tax rates and even exemption.

China should make sensible use of price policy and stabilize the prices of agricultural products through stable production. a. The government should determine the objective prices or the lowest protection prices so as to guide the market prices of agricultural products, accelerate the production of major agricultural products and raise the rural income levels. b. China should develop a futures market for agricultural products, and set up long-term mechanisms to guarantee the stable production and sales of agricultural products.

China should make use of the policies concerning the import and export of agricultural products, bring into full play the comparative advantages of agriculture and regulate domestic supply of and demand for agricultural products. a. The Chinese market for agricultural products should pay attention to linking up with the international market, agricultural resources should be deployed in light of comparative advantages, and the export of agricultural products with comparative advantages should be spurred to obtain the maximum economic returns. The government should adopt various policies to give sturdy support for the export of agricultural products, encourage rural enterprises and rural economic organizations to export such products directly, distribute export quotas by public bidding, and subsidize agricultural exports if necessary. b. The state should make full use of the import and export trade mechanisms to regulate the domestic supply of and demand for agricultural products.

(IV) The Key to the Reform of the Circulation System of Agricultural Products Lies in the Realization of the Diversification and Liberalization of Competitive Principals

To realize the marketization of the rural economy, the circulation field must achieve diversification and liberalization among the competitive principals so as to enable rural households and enterprises to enter the market, select business partners and set prices on their own.

We must create diversified competitive market principals in the circulation of agricultural commodities, getting rid of the market monopoly of a handful of departments and units. Except for the supply and marketing cooperatives, each circulation link of agricultural products and means of agricultural production should develop a large number of economic cooperative organizations in individual, privately-owned, state-owned and other forms. The supply and marketing cooperatives may be, and can only be, one of the business partners of the farmers. If the farmers think that business with the supply and marketing cooperative does not tally with their own interests, they may switch to doing business with other commercial organizations.

The reform of supply and marketing cooperatives in rural areas should be further deepened. These bodies should restore their original collective ownership in an all-round way, and should be managed in accordance with the cooperative principle, so as to make them commercial organizations promoting the farmers' interests. They should provide means of production to farmers at lower prices and offer higher prices for their produce than other bodies. Only in this way can the farmers regard supply and marketing cooperatives as their own enterprises. While the supply and marketing cooperatives are being reformed and their collective ownership is being restored, they should be operated and managed in strict accordance with the principle of collective ownership so that they can play more active roles in protecting farmers' incomes and promoting rural

WESTERN CHINA'S RESOURCE EXPLOITATION BY SPECIAL ECONOMIC ZONES

CHAPTER III MARKETIZATION OF PURCHASE AND SALES SYSTEMS

economic development. After the supply and marketing cooperatives restore collective ownership the system of integrated cooperatives above the county level should be changed correspondingly. All provincial supply and marketing cooperatives and the All-China Federation of Supply and Marketing Cooperatives are economic organizations belonging to the farmers rather than government organs.

At present, most agricultural products in China are circulated according to the internal demands of the market economy. For instance, peasants now feel free to sell vegetables, fruits, meat, domestic fowls and eggs in the market, selecting buyers and setting prices on their own. Only some primary agricultural products, such as grain, cotton and oil-bearing crops, are purchased according to the state purchase-by-order system. These primary products occupy a very important position in the national economy and the people's livelihood, and involve the supply of materials for thousands of households' daily life and the supply of basic raw materials to urban light and textile industries. At present, shortages of these agricultural products have not been fundamentally eradicated, the reform of state-owned enterprises in cities has not been completed, and the state's macroeconomic control has not been perfected. Under these circumstances, it is necessary for the state to purchase primary agricultural products by the state according to contracts. So when enterprises or private individuals purchase primary agricultural and sideline products at higher prices in violation of the state's policies and decrees they should be firmly punished.

In view of the needs of the long-term development of the rural market economy, there exist some internal contradictions in the state's system of purchasing primary agricultural products by order. First, it constitutes a buyer's monopoly, and hence denies to the farmers autonomous status in the market. In the countries with advanced market economies governments purchase agricultural products at protection prices, which are higher than market prices, rather than purchasing them according to contracts. The adoption of protection prices, which does not deny farmers autonomy, will not dampen their enthusiasm for production. Second, the state's purchase of agricultural products by contract is a form of direct control implemented by the sectors with a low level of socialization of production, which runs counter to the ordinary rules of macroeconomic control. Under current conditions, the level of socialized production of the iron and steel, coal, chemical, machinery, textiles and construction materials industries in urban areas is higher than that of agriculture. Since the reform started, most planned allocation of these products has been abolished, and control of their production and circulation has been lifted and their production and circulation have been allowed to be regulated by the market. This proves that such reform does no harm to the regulation and stability of the macroeconomy. But it is theoretically impossible for direct control of the circulation of agricultural products with a low level of production socialization over a long period of time. Third, the production period of agricultural products is comparatively long and the current year's market prices will affect the following year's output. The "spider's web" theory of modern economics tells us that pure market regulation of agricultural products may give rise to huge fluctuations. Therefore, the production and circulation of agricultural products needs some degree of government intervention. International experience also tells us that there are various ways in which governments can intervene in the process of production and sale of agricultural products: Setting up risk funds for primary agricultural products; increasing state grain storage; increasing the amount of agricultural products purchased by the state when the country has bumper harvests and increasing the sales of agricultural products from the national storehouses when there the harvests are poor; increasing the government's investment in agricultural infrastructure facilities, etc. Without directly interfering in farmers' production and sales activities, the government may also effectively balance the market supply and demand, and realize macroeconomic coordination and stability. Fourth, the state purchase of agricultural products by order subordinates farms to urban enterprises. Since the reform started urban enterprises have gradually gained more autonomy. They may enter the market more freely, and select business partners and set prices on

CHAPTER III MARKETIZATION OF PURCHASE AND SALES SYSTEMS

their own. In this way their independent status as principals in the market is basically realized. Along with the further deepening of the reform of enterprises, this trend will become more obvious. In addition, state purchase of agricultural products by order prevents the farmers from being able to fully exercise their autonomy in the circulation field. Especially in periods of inflation, enterprises may ensure optimum economic returns through selecting business partners by themselves and fixing prices on their own. But farmers can only sell their products to the state at fixed prices, and have to purchase what they need from urban enterprises at market prices. More often than not, this is one of the important reasons why income differences between urban and rural residents become aggravated, enthusiasm for investing in agricultural production gets dampened and the migration of rural labor into the cities speeds up. Finally, the state purchase of primary agricultural products by order is actually the traditional socialist capital accumulation. The state-set prices for agricultural products purchased by order are often lower than the market balance prices. However the sales prices of enterprises specializing in trading in primary agricultural products may be close to the market prices, the profit from which may form sources of capital for the country's construction. If it sells agricultural products in cities at prices lower than the market prices, the government reduces the wage and raw material costs of urban enterprises, which will result in the rapid development of urban industries and commerce and quickly increase the state's financial income. This is none other than the primitive accumulation method of the traditional planned economy. Practice proves that this primitive accumulation method will often result in backward rural economic development and form a lopsided binary national economic structure. But in this situation the state can not compulsorily use exchange of unequal values to absorb agricultural surpluses. Instead, the state should gradually increase the input into agriculture, guide modern industries in urban areas to support agriculture, and accumulate construction capital through standardized taxation, government bonds, financial deposits and profits handed in by state-owned enterprises, rather than mobilize capital by means of the traditional accumulation method. Therefore, further research is needed to decide whether the circulation of primary agricultural products is best served by continuing the system of state purchase by order or by lifting controls in an appropriate manner; and if the modern circulation system should be overhauled at an appropriate time when the shortage of agricultural products is further alleviated, urban enterprise reform is further deepened and the state's indirect macro regulation and control are further perfected.

Along with the development of the rural market economy, the factors that restrain the development of agriculture have been transferred from the production field to the circulation field, i.e., from the market being decided by the production to the production being decided by the market. Hence we must strengthen our concept of the market, deepen the reform of the circulation system for agricultural products, and set up and perfect a unified market system, including products, labor, capital, land and other key production elements. In particular, we should speed up the construction of markets of key elements which have been stagnant, and encourage collectives and individuals to participate in circulation in order to create a situation in which millions of people are engaged in circulation. Markets of all kinds should be open, competitive and standardized. Here "open" means open to the outside world in an all-round way without being restricted to within the boundaries of counties, cities, provinces or countries; "competitive" refers to creating conditions for fair, just and open competition in the market and improving economic vitality through competition. To perfect the market system China must foster a variety of market principals. Except for carrying out structural reform in state-owned commerce, grain and foreign trade enterprises and supply and marketing cooperatives, China should give farmers autonomy and the power to construct, enter and make use of markets.

CHAPTER III MARKETIZATION OF PURCHASE AND SALES SYSTEMS

II. Grain Policies and Supply and Demand

(I) The Evolution of the Policies Concerning the Purchase and Marketing of Grain

Of all the agricultural policies those on the purchase and marketing of grain occupy an extremely important position. In the early 1990s China made big advances in the reform of the grain purchase and marketing system. In early 1992 the central government put forward the principle of reforming the grain purchase and marketing system featured by "each province making decisions, and each region carrying out the reform on its own." Guangdong Province took the lead in lifting the control of grain selling prices. By the end of 1993 over 98 percent of counties and cities throughout the country had lifted controls from grain prices. But three problems soon cropped up: a. The localities only lifted control from marketing prices, but not purchase prices. b. After the control of grain marketing prices was lifted China did not make it clear in time who had the ownership of the grain which was being purchased by order, thus providing enterprises engaged in purchase and marketing grain with an opportunity to buy grain at low prices and sell it again at high prices. c. The reason why control of grain prices was lifted so rapidly was that the governments at all levels hoped to reduce the amount of financial subsidies. As a matter of fact, the reform could only be carried out at that time, when there was plenty of grain and the government's purchase prices were very close to the market prices, but the reform found it difficult to withstand the fluctuations in the relations between the supply of and demand for grain. At the end of 1993 grain prices on the market rose rapidly, and tremendous changes took place in the situation. To prevent the price situation turning from bad to worse, the central government adopted five important measures: a. It was specified that state-owned grain stores had to sell some kinds of grain at government-fixed prices. b. The buying prices of grain purchased by the state according to contracts was to be raised. In 1994 the purchasing prices of grain set by the state were 40 percent higher than those of the previous year. c. It was made clear that state-owned grain sectors should command more grain resources. Except for purchasing 100 billion *jin* (1 *jin* = 0.5 kg) of grain according to contracts, they had to purchase 80 billion *jin* of grain at negotiated prices. d. The state's reserve grain was used, and by the end of 1994 some 29 billion *jin* of reserved grain had been used. e. Local governments were allowed to give subsidies for grain purchased by order, depending on concrete conditions.

Problems appearing in the purchase and sale of grain in 1994 were as follows: First, some localities did not implement the State Council's specifications on purchasing grain at negotiated prices according to the market conditions. Instead, they fixed grain prices on their own and assigned grain purchasing at fixed prices to the farmers. Second, some localities violated the specifications made by the State Council by closing down grain markets so as to lower local grain prices. Third, some organs of the state-owned grain sector speculated in grain purchased by the state according to contracts. It is worth finding out whether these problems are a result of human error or are basic flaws in the system; if the former, they can be corrected by readjusting policies, but in case of the latter a reform of the system is imperative.

It is worth seriously considering the problems which have cropped up in implementing grain purchase and marketing policies:

1. We should not develop the economy at the expense of agriculture. In 1994 the overheated growth of grain prices was an objective cause of such problems. Therefore, the first question to be answered is, why did grain prices constantly rise in 1994? The decline in rice supply was the main cause. As compared with 1984, in 1994 China's population had risen by 15 percent. However, the output of rice decreased by 0.9 percent. In the past 10 years China's total grain output has increased by 9.2 percent, of which wheat output increased by 16.0 percent and corn, by 34.0 percent. But rice decreased by 0.9 percent. As 92 percent of China's rice output is contributed by south China, the decrease of rice output was actually a reduction in grain output in south China. It is worth thinking about what the connection is between

CHAPTER III MARKETIZATION OF PURCHASE AND SALES SYSTEMS

the decline in grain output and the rapid economic growth in south China. It is an extremely dangerous trend that some places seek economic growth at the expense of agriculture, grain production in particular. One of the things which gave birth to this trend was the imbalance between local governments' responsibility for economic construction and their responsibility to provide grain.

2. The grain controlled by the state-owned grain sector, especially the grain controlled by each of its branches, is equivalent neither to the grain controlled by the local government, nor to the grain controlled by the central government, and this is the inevitable result of divergence of interests among the principals in the reform.

The grain sector and its branches have their own independent interests, and so unless the functions of the government are separated from those of the grain sector we can hardly rely on the grain sector to manage the grain market.

3. The functions of the state purchase of grain by order should be clearly recognized. As the prices of grain purchased by the government are generally lower than the market prices it is inevitable that the government finds it difficult to buy high-quality grain. The grain purchased by the state is mainly stored as a hedge against wars and disasters. It is also used to guarantee grain supplies to people with low incomes. In addition, these stockpiles can play a part in stabilizing the prices of forage and of grain for industrial use, although they can have no effect on the prices of the fine-quality grain consumed by most people.

4. The policies favor those with low incomes. In view of consumers' resilience shown when grain prices rose in 1994, the conditions are ripe for supplying grain subsidies to those with low incomes.

Since 1995 each provincial government has taken all-round responsibility for local grain production, purchase, marketing, circulation between provinces, market control, storage and handling, under what is known as the "provincial governor responsibility system." This is an important measure that China has taken for the improvement of the grain purchase and marketing system. There is no doubt that it marks important progress as compared with the situation in which the central government was responsible for feeding everyone in the country. The new system helps the implementation of the principle of "having enough to eat first and carrying out construction later." All local governments are urged to attach importance to grain production, to bring into play each locality's comparative advantages, and gradually form a national unified grain market. It is obvious that the implementation of this system is not aimed at carrying out isolated self-sufficiency in grain, but at realizing grain circulation and the balance of supply and demand among regions by making full use of the role of the market. Special attention must be paid to the decline in grain output among the main grain producers, the wastage of grain in transition and regional isolation. There are two prominent issues at present: The first is the reform of the state-owned grain sector. We must realistically admit that if we can not satisfy the immediate interests of the 3.6 million people employed in the state-owned grain sector, the reform of the grain purchase and marketing system can hardly be carried out smoothly. The second concerns the relations between the farmers and the market. Scattered farm households which operate on an extremely small scale can not directly enter the national unified grain market. Moreover, the government has no way to coordinate the operations of over 200 million peasant households scattered all over the country. Therefore, to develop intermediate organizations linking peasant households and the market will be an indispensable basic task in the course of the gradual development and perfection of China's grain and other agricultural product markets.

(II) Balanced Interests: The Solid Foundation for Grain to Advance Steadily Toward the Market

Following the institution of the rural reform in the early 1980s, more than 90 percent of the counties and cities in China have lifted control over grain purchase and marketing prices, and the overwhelming majority of cities have abolished control over the prices of most non-staple foodstuffs. The marketization of the grain business has become an inevitable and irreversible trend.

As China has achieved bumper harvests several years run-

CHAPTER III MARKETIZATION OF PURCHASE AND SALES SYSTEMS

ning, and supply and demand are basically balanced. This balance —both balanced total amount and balanced interests—is the foundation stone for the gradual marketization of the grain sector.

Balanced interests refer to the principle that the income of grain producers should be equivalent to the income of producers of other items, both agricultural and non-agricultural, in the countryside. Only if a balance of interests is realized can we eliminate the phenomenon of grave distortion between grain prices and the prices of other industrial and agricultural products, and make grain prices truly reflect the supply of and demand for grain commodities. In this way we may stabilize the enthusiasm of grain producers and enable grain to enter the market step by step.

1. The unitary agricultural production structure.

Agriculture plays a leading role in the national economic production structure, and grain growing is the mainstay crop. Governments at all levels have stressed time and again the importance of agriculture, and especially the importance of grain. Whether a locality's grain output or growing area has reached the standard has become the yardstick with which to measure the performance of local officials. The stability of the total amount of grain is realized at the cost of the development of other industries, and so the unitary agricultural production structure is the first and foremost reason why many agricultural areas all over China are relatively poor.

2. Low economic returns from growing grain.

As the total grain output is taken as the standard for checking agricultural achievements, the farmers have to raise grain output at all costs, such as by compulsory replacement with natural resources and capital. In order to create "one ton of grain per-*mu*," and "exemplary fields," and increase grain output, the governments and farmers in some commodity grain bases had paid high costs, hence the appearance of poor counties and townships with high grain output. Such a situation still existed in the main grain production areas at the beginning of the 1990s. For instance, in over 200 counties with net per capita income

105

exceeding 1,000 yuan in 1992, not a single one is located in the main grain, cotton or oil-bearing crop production areas, such as Hubei, Hunan, Jiangxi and Anhui.

3. Ignoring the improvement of quality.

Attaching the utmost importance to the output of agricultural products was realistic for quite a long historical period. However, seeking the mere increase of quantity resulted in stagnant quality. If we judge agricultural development in terms of the total quantity of grain, the following three errors tend to crop up: a. An irrational grain structure. For instance, the grain output in 1993 was a historic high. But as the areas sown with paddy rice dropped sharply by 26.42 million *mu*, the rice output shrank by more than 20 billion *jin*, which led to an increase in rice prices. Consequently, the per capita supply of rice in south China, with a total population of 663 million, (the main rice-eating area in the country) dropped by over 30 *jin* on average; and the prices of rice rose sharply, which propelled the growth of prices of other commodities. b. Though the grain output was high, the quality was low. For instance, peasants grew more polished long-grained nonglutinous rice than round-grained nonglutinous rice. c. People blindly expanded the production of famous, special and fine quality products by means of inputting chemical fertilizers, pesticides and inorganic materials, thus turning out many unorthodox products. As a result, they gradually lost market competitiveness.

4. Blindly exploiting natural resources and ignoring ecological protection.

Driven by the need to increase production at all costs, units engaged in agriculture have attached great importance to means for intensifying labor, such as improving output by increasing the multiple-crop index, and amounts of pesticides and chemical fertilizers, and ignoring measures for the self-development and self-protection of the agricultural ecology. Consequently, the soil has often become hardened and impervious, and crops have deteriorated and become polluted. The exhaustion of the agricultural ecology means that a favorable circulation and a balanced system can hardly be realized.

CHAPTER III MARKETIZATION OF PURCHASE AND SALES SYSTEMS

5. The trend toward intensifying the interest contradictions among the state, collectives and individuals.

With the introduction of the market economy, farmers tended to concentrate on production which would maximize their incomes. The result was a turning away from grain, which promised only moderate monetary returns. This posed a problem for the collectives, which had the characteristic of integrating the functions of the government with those of the producers. In order to perform the functions of the government, the collectives adopted various means, integrating rewards with punishments to get the farmers to fulfill their state-mandated grain quotas. However, whenever the control was relaxed in this respect the collectives would try to shuffle off responsibility for grain deliveries. Hence the objectives of the state, collectives and individuals were totally different, and quantity fluctuated.

6. Stress on total quantity balance may alienate the producers.

The balance of total quantity is temporary and relative; when the supply is larger than the demand grain operation sectors will, more often than not, refuse to purchase or purchase at low prices, or even vie with each other in selling stored grain. The farmers then suffer losses by selling grain at low prices.

After the founding of New China in 1949 the government took the balanced total quantity as the signal that it could relax control over grain. Such a guiding ideology, ignoring farmers' interests and adopting policies favoring urban and industrial interests over those of the countryside, was reflected in the practice of guiding agricultural production. China has always paid attention to the increase of grain output but ignored the protection of the agricultural ecology. Such methods, which prevailed in the era of the planned economy, produced sharp contradictions when agriculture encountered the market economy, and so now China's agriculture is in a difficult position.

(III) Analysis of the Factors Affecting China's Grain Production

The fundamental factors affecting the total grain output are the per *mu* yield and size of sown areas. Hence, if grain output is to be increased, then the per *mu* yield must be increased and the grain-sown area must be expanded, or at least stabilized.

From 1952 to 1993 the area of arable land nationwide shrank from 1,619 million *mu* to 1,425 million *mu*, or a decrease of 12 percent. But the growth of the multiple-crop index canceled out the negative effects of the decline. According to statistics, the total sown area of grain crops shrank from 1.86 billion *mu* in 1952 to 1.67 billion *mu* in 1993, or a decrease of 190 million *mu*, or 10.2 percent. Comparing the quantities of grain-sown areas and total grain output, the enlargement of the sown areas between the 1950s and the 1960s played an important role in raising the total output. But later the increase of the total grain output was mainly due to the growth of per *mu* yield. According to statistics, from 1952 to 1993 the per *mu* yield of grain went up from 88 kg to 275 kg, or an increase of 4.6 kg annually. The rise of per *mu* yield of grain was the decisive factor behind the six-stage growth of total grain output. However, the growth of per *mu* yield was mainly due to the improvement of the state's policies and measures, the increase of material input into agriculture and the combination of these two aspects.

1. Analysis of material and technical conditions.

Material and technical conditions are the key elements affecting per *mu* yield of grain, and the key to increasing grain output. These conditions refer to the input of materials and capital and the application of science and technology.

(1) Increase in input is the basic guarantee of the increase of grain output.

Input mainly refers to the input of materials, capital and labor. The input of materials and labor is the decisive factor for increasing grain output, and the input of capital strengthens the motive power for further development.

The role of the input of farm-use materials, such as chemical fertilizers, is obvious. Between 1952 and 1993 the consumption of chemical fertilizers increased from 300,000 tons to 154.11 million tons, or an increase of 3.5 million tons annually on average (converted into 710,000 tons of net chemical fertilizers). This

CHAPTER III MARKETIZATION OF PURCHASE AND SALES SYSTEMS

means that for an increase of 50 billion kg of grain, 21.33 million tons of chemical fertilizers (converted into 4.36 million tons of net chemical fertilizers) needed to be added, 52.4 billion watt of farm machinery motive power (or an increase of 7.6 billion watt annually on average), and 20.3 billion kwh of electricity (or an increase of 2.9 kwh annually on average). According to the State Statistics Bureau, in stable conditions an increase of 1 kg of chemical fertilizers might lead to an increase of 7-10 kg of grain. According to the Study of China's Comprehensive Agricultural Production Capacity, the average contribution rates of various key elements—chemical fertilizers, draft animals, plastic sheeting, pesticides, farm machinery and improved varieties—to grain output were, respectively, 32 percent, 6.3 percent, 2.5 percent, 3.8 percent, 10.9 percent and 16.2 percent.

Capital investment is the necessary condition for reinforcing agricultural infrastructure facilities and the guarantee of the increase of grain output. According to statistics, financial assistance for agriculture, investment in agricultural capital construction, and the year-end remaining sum of agricultural loans increased respectively from 270 million yuan, 580 million yuan and 320 million yuan in 1952 to 40 billion yuan, 13.1 billion yuan and 211.1 billion yuan in 1993, or average annual growths of respectively 970 million yuan, 310 million and 5.1 billion yuan. Since the Seventh Five-Year Plan period (1988-1992), along with the reform of the state's investment system, a new multi-level, multi-channel and multi-form setup for the agricultural investment system has been formed. This system played an important role in mitigating the fluctuations in grain production during the Seventh Five-Year Plan period and helping reach an annual output of 450 billion kg. In the five years from 1988 to 1992 the government, localities and farmers invested 20 billion yuan in the comprehensive development of agriculture, upgraded more than 100 million *mu* of fields with low and medium-level yields, opened more than 15 million *mu* of waste land and raised the grain-production capacity by an additional 17 billion kg. In addition, through joint investment by the government and localities, 500 state-level commodity grain bases were constructed, which made a 20 percent contribution to the increase of grain output from 400 billion kg to 450 billion kg. This proves that the investment in agriculture has a great effect on the production of grain.

In addition, the improvement of agricultural infrastructure facilities such as water conservancy is an effective measure to improve agriculture's capacity to resist natural disasters. Between 1952 and 1993 the effective irrigated area increased from 299 million *mu* to 729 million *mu*, and, on average, the production of every additional 50 billion *jin* of grain needed an increase of 71.67 million *mu* of effective irrigated area, or an average annual growth of 10.49 million *mu*. The proportion of effective irrigated area in the arable land increased from 18.5 percent in 1952 to 51.2 percent in 1993. Research indicates that between 1985 and 1990 irrigation made a 28.1 percent contribution to the increase of grain output. The increase in effective irrigated area not only made up for the unfavorable impact of the reduction in arable land on the increase of grain output, but also played an important role in improving the cultivated area and in reinforcing agriculture's capacity to withstand natural disasters.

It has been estimated that it took 14 years to increase the total grain output from 150 billion kg to 200 billion kg. Moreover, the average annual growth in the application of chemical fertilizer was 880,000 tons (converted into 180,000 tons of net chemical fertilizer), that of electricity consumed in rural areas 400 million kwh, that of financial expenditure 1.5 billion yuan, and that of the investment in agricultural capital construction 1.8 billion yuan. It only took two years to increase the total grain output from 350 billion kg to 400 billion kg, and the average annual increase of chemical fertilizer came to 3.42 million tons (converted into 700,000 tons of net chemical fertilizer), that of electricity consumed in rural areas 3.4 billion kwh, that of financial expenditure 8.6 billion yuan, and that of the investment in agricultural capital construction 3.2 billion yuan. These figures verify that the higher the increase of the annual input, the quicker the increase in grain production, and vice versa.

(2) Progress in science and technology is the key to increasing

CHAPTER III MARKETIZATION OF PURCHASE AND SALES SYSTEMS

grain output.

During the 1950s and the 1960s China promoted the planting of high-yield crops, reformed the farming system and spread short-stalk paddy rice. In the 1980s the promotion of hybrid rice, hybrid maize and other improved varieties of crops, and agricultural technologies such as the use of plastic sheeting, mixed fertilizers, model-type cultivation, and comprehensive prevention and treatment of plant diseases and insect pests played an important role in increasing grain output and reaching the level of 450 billion kg of grain. Research indicates that during the Seventh Five-Year Plan period the contribution made by the progress in agricultural technology accounted for 30.43 percent to the increase in grain output.

2. Analysis of social and economic conditions.

Grain production in China is inevitably affected by social and economic conditions, and by comparative economic returns and the roles of policy factors in particular.

(1) If farmers can obtain more economic returns from growing grain than from planting other crops (including fruit trees), they will be enthusiastic about growing grain. So the grain sown areas will not decrease, and the grain output will not be greatly affected. The past few years have shown that due to low economic returns from growing grain, both economically developed and developing areas have preferred to reduce grain-sown areas and expand the areas of cash crops. Some areas in south China urged the local farmers to grow grain only for their own consumption and to aim for prosperity in only three years by developing orchards. In particular, the grain production of the coastal areas in southeast China has declined because of the low economic returns from growing grain. According to statistics, the proportion of grain output of 14 provinces, autonomous regions and municipalities directly under the central government in south China shrank from 58.3 percent of the country's total in 1989 to 52.7 percent in 1993, or a decrease of five percent. However, Liaoning, a province which had been short of grain for quite a long time, realized a balanced gross grain output by employing various means (such as irrigated rice fields and increase of the

multiple cropping area).

(2) The role of government policies in increasing grain output.

Agricultural development "depends first on science and second on policies." This is even truer of grain production. From the aspect of the six stages China has passed through in its agricultural development, each stage is related to a policy readjustment, especially the fourth and fifth stages, i.e., from 1978 to 1984, when grain output increased from 300 billion kg to 400 billion kg. Government policies played a very important role in these six years, spanning two stages. During this period the implementation of the contract responsibility system based on the household, with remuneration linked to output, in an all-round way and massive rises in the purchasing prices of grain became direct impetuses for mobilizing the farmers' enthusiasm for developing grain production. Some experts estimate that between 1978 and 1984 these policies contributed 40 percent to the increase of grain output. Given good material conditions, government policies are the key factor in the improvement of comprehensive grain production capacity. However, for a long time the state's policies favored heavy industry at the expense of agriculture, resulting in tense relations between industry and agriculture and unbalanced development proportions that hindered the increase of grain output.

(IV) The Current Weak Grain Market Is Related to Inefficient Market, Passive Government and Inactive Farmers

Any actions by the government or farmers running counter to the market will be detrimental to the reform of the grain production system. At the moment, the marketization of agriculture has just started, and there exist many contradictions and obvious problems. There have always been difficulties in marketizing grain products, manifested in passive government and inactive farmers, and causing great fluctuations in production. If we regard agricultural marketization as merely lifting control from prices and operations, the market will spin out of control and a vicious circle will emerge as the government is forced to

CHAPTER III MARKETIZATION OF PURCHASE AND SALES SYSTEMS

impose controls again. Thus, the constant change from control to chaos and back again will hamper the growth of the market.

1. Disordered Market.

Grain products themselves have weak commodity characteristics. More often than not, pure market regulation can not work properly. Grain products are low-quality items with both natural and market risks. Growing grain is a basic occupation with small economic returns for the producer but large economic returns for society as a whole, making it difficult to stabilize the market.

(1) Grain has a low commodity rate. The grain market's growth depends on the amount of grain available on the market rather than the total output of grain. The agricultural population makes up 80 percent of China's total. So grain is first of all produced to meet the demand from China's rural people. At present, China's grain commodity rate is only about 36 percent, of which a part is realized through purchase by order. This is not commodity exchange in the strict sense.

(2) The elasticity of demand for grain is small, while that of grain supply is large. Grain is the most basic of people's daily necessities. Therefore, when grain prices go up consumption will not be greatly restrained, and when prices fall the direct consumption of grain will not increase greatly, either. However, the elasticity of grain supply is fairly large, which is mainly reflected in the fact that when grain prices go up the farmers will be encouraged to grow grain, but when grain prices fall they will reduce their output. When analyzing the characteristics of grain supply we must pay attention to two characteristics: a. The period it takes for supply to reflect output is fairly long, usually more than a year. b. The supply includes two concepts—the production amount and the commodity amount. In general, the elasticity of grain supply is large, followed by the elasticity of production.

(3) The economic returns from grain production are low, both from the comparative (with other crops) and household income points of view. The reasons are that China has a large population, comparatively little arable land, an oversupply of rural labor and too many small-scale farming households. The latter favor high-interest industries or products, i.e., by putting

the major elements of production into projects with high economic returns, while stabilizing self-supply production and taking up smaller economic opportunities. Both economic and sociological factors thus make grain growing relatively insensitive to market signals. In addition, the areas sown with grain will not fluctuate in size sharply as compared to those sown with other crops. When grain prices rise farmers do not invest their family's major elements of production in grain, nor do they greatly reduce the areas sown with grain when prices fall. This is because the self-supply production part, which is relatively isolated from the market, is comparatively stable and guaranteed. Therefore, as market regulation does not work properly it is impossible to solve China's grain problem by only raising prices.

2. The passive government.

Unlike in the case of other commodities, the consumption and production of grain can not be automatically regulated by means of the "unseen hand" of market forces. The alleviation of the contradictions between the supply of and demand for grain is closely related to fundamental improvements in macro environmental conditions, including the government's support for agriculture, the reinforcement of agricultural investment, the improvement of infrastructure facilities and the operation of farmers' organizations. One of the most difficult tasks in the national reform is how to work out appropriate policies and develop the rural market in light of the grain market's own laws and producers' and consumers' interests. The weakness of the grain market is related to mistakes by the government in the following four aspects:

(1) Low ability to store grain and to transform grain into other products. At present, there exists a distorted situation in which some places seriously lack grain while other places have surplus grain. Due to out-of-date equipment for grain storage, difficulties in transporting grain, and low capacity for processing grain, many farming areas, especially some grain-producing areas, have difficulties in selling, storing, transporting and processing grains. Also, difficulties in purchasing and selling grain appear periodically.

CHAPTER III MARKETIZATION OF PURCHASE AND SALES SYSTEMS

(2) Poor interest insurance mechanisms. In the past few years many farming areas in China have had bumper harvests of grain. However, due to a sharp decline in negotiated prices and listed market prices, farmers can not earn as much from grain as they should, and a sharp contrast between the growth of grain output and low economic returns has appeared. In years of poor harvests the state resumes monopolized operation, with narrow circulation channels, which prevents grain which is in short supply earning its true value. In addition, grain production itself lacks self-regulation mechanisms, so that farmers' interests can not be effectively guaranteed.

(3) Low degree of organization in the grain market. The organization of China's grain market is very weak. Except for the central, provincial and municipal levels, the purchasing, storage, transportation and sales networks necessary for regulating the market are still in embryonic form. In particular, as the futures market is not developed, farmers can not receive long- and medium-term price signals. Moreover, the government may raise or reduce grain prices at any time, so the farmers are constantly unsure about grain prices and are reluctant to enter the circulation field directly.

(4) The low degree of development of the market system. At present, problems such as unhealthy development, poor infrastructure facilities, and irrational and monolithic structure are commonly seen in the grain market, especially in the rural grain market. In terms of transport, communications, posts and telecommunications, finance, information and other vital links, the rural grain market lags far behind cities and other economic sectors. The result is that it can not meet the demands of agricultural development, which is become more commercialized and modernized day by day.

3. Negative attitudes among the farmers.

The marketization of agriculture should be an extremely precious opportunity for rural people to become prosperous. However, the chaotic market has caused losses for the farmers, and without effective support from the government, they instinctively stick to the natural economy for security and adopt a negative attitude toward entering the market. As the main force for deepening the rural reform is the farmers, so long as they play their roles in the market they can support the rapid growth of the whole national economy. However, scattered rural household production is not conducive to meeting market demand and farmers can not get timely and accurate information on demand and supply. In general, profitable production may easily turn into stagnation. At the same time, quite a number of rural people who still harbor a sense of the desirability of self-sufficiency and small-scale peasant economy, form a social force which instinctively resists the market and is isolated from the outside world, thus increasing the isolation from the market of grain production. The farmers find it hard to understand the rules of large-scale socialized production, the fierce fluctuations touched off by the relations between market supply and demand. They also find it hard to understand the roles of interest mechanisms. Consequently, efforts to reform the grain price system may cause social unrest in the countryside.

(V) Farmers' Expectations of Grain Price Increases Directly Affect Market Grain Prices

The main causes of the rise of grain prices in 1993, when China's grain output grew at the highest rate ever, were as follows: In 1992 the government adopted important reform measures such as abolishing the state monopoly of supply and marketing in the countryside and abolishing grain coupons in cities. Due to the former measure, Guangdong, Fujian, Zhejiang, Jiangsu and other coastal provinces reduced grain production, as grain had lost its comparative advantage and they wished to decrease their subsidies for grain production. East China needed more grain from central China, leading to a rise of grain prices in the latter region. The local governments in central China adopted measures to isolate the grain market in order to sustain local grain prices. As a result, as east China ran short of grain the price of grain in east China went up by a large margin.

In view of the great fluctuations of the prices on the grain markets in the past few years, the government calls on all locali-

CHAPTER III MARKETIZATION OF PURCHASE AND SALES SYSTEMS

ties to attach great importance to grain production, stabilize the areas sown with grain, and increase investment in agricultural infrastructure facilities. The analysis in the previous paragraph points out that the sharp rises of grain prices after 1993 should not be attributed to a fall in grain production. Therefore, the increase of grain output may not stabilize grain prices on the market. Even if the growth of grain output stabilizes grain prices on the market, many side-effects will appear. In particular, if the economically advanced coastal areas increase their grain output they will need less grain from central China. Then grain prices in central China will not rise and the incomes of peasants in the grain-growing areas of central China will stagnate, delaying any solution to the problems of the farmers' living standards and income differences among regions.

(VI) We Should Give Priority to Balanced Total Grain Output

Grain is a basic daily-life commodity. Therefore, when observing the effects of the reform of the grain supply and marketing system we should not only pay attention to the scale and degree to which grain enters the market economy. Instead, we should determine whether this process can promote the stability and improvement of China's balanced total grain output and create a favorable environment for the reform of China's economic system as a whole and the sustained development of the national economy. If we push grain production and circulation to the market in an all-round way, this will be at the cost of the balanced total grain output and shows that conditions in China are not yet mature enough for this.

In recent years grain prices have fluctuated constantly, a fact which has made people pay more attention to the importance of a total balanced grain output. More and more people have come to understand the weakness of China's total balanced grain output and have understood the great significance of keeping a balance in the total grain amount to the economy, society and politics. The balance of the structure of grain for supply and demand is also an important task, but it can be accomplished only on the basis of a balanced total grain amount. Of course, the policy of "high yield, fine quality and high efficiency" is also applicable to grain production and supply. But while implementing the policy in an all-round way, we must firmly stick to the premise of "high yield."

The great fluctuations of grain prices have taught us two important lessons in terms of the balance of total grain output: First, it is important to achieve a balance of the total quantity within a large area or region; it is not enough to simply balance the nation's total grain output. Within quite a long period of time a comparatively large region should have its own balanced total quantity. Some economically advanced areas put undue emphasis on seeking economic returns from the disposition of land resources by reducing the area of grain fields, but they then have to rely on other areas to make up their shortages of grain. Advanced areas must have their own advanced grain production systems. Second, it is imperative to raise the balance of the total amount of major grain varieties. As to primary grain varieties, such as rice, wheat and corn, we must work for a basic balance between their supply and demand. Though one variety of grain may replace another to meet the demand of consumers, experience has proved that the possibility of such replacement is fairly small. However, supplies of major kinds of grain which are in short supply have great influence on the prices at the grain market. The mutually contradictory fluctuating mechanisms in the market warn people to pay adequate attention to the balance between supply of and demand for major grain varieties.

The balanced total grain amount affects production as well as circulation. Without purchase, storage, processing, allocation, regulation, transportation and marketing grain can not be transferred from producers to consumers. Moreover, the contradictions between urban and rural areas, between regions, between seasons in terms of producing and marketing grain, and between supply and demand can hardly be solved in an orderly way without the above processes being carried out smoothly. More important is the fact that in a market economy methods of grain circulation and the formation of prices decide the interests of grain producers and consumers. Therefore, the reform of the purchase and marketing systems, and changes in price levels and price proportions—important contents of the state's macro regulation and control—necessitate attention to the interests of business people, producers and consumers alike.

(VII) Actively Cultivating the Principals in Grain Circulation

The establishment of circulation principals is the foundation for the construction of grain circulation organizations and is also the key link for the state to exercise macro control of the circulation of grain. In general, the market economy system requires that, except for state regulation and control organizations, the principal operation entities of circulation should be run as enterprises.

In view of China's current situation, while setting up the principals of grain circulation we should put stress on the following three points:

First is the necessity to separate the state grain storage and regulation sector from the operation sector.

These two sectors have different, even contrasting, objectives. When they are integrated the regulation and control sector's objectives are often constrained, replaced or damaged by the operation sector's concentration on obtaining profits. At the end of 1994 the fact that abnormal fluctuations of grain prices in China were not restrained in time but were immediately put under control after the state adopted measures fully proves the contradictions between the profit-winning objectives and control objectives of the integrated grain sectors.

Second, the state's grain operation sector's role should be brought into full play. When the grain amount is balanced, state grain enterprises, with their national network are very important circulation levers.

Third, we must adhere to a multi-element and multi-channel setup in terms of grain circulation. When control by the state grain operation sector is lifted, individual, private and cooperative economies should be allowed to enter the business of grain circulation, and develop multi-channel operations so as to accelerate the formation of market stimulating and restraining mechanisms, reduce circulation costs, improve circulation efficiency and speed up the reform of the state grain operation sector. Control of the purchase of grain from farmers should be lifted and competition should be allowed. So long as the state grants the farmers autonomy to fix prices their enthusiasm for growing grain can be assured and sufficient grain supplies can be guaranteed. When the supply of grain falls short of demand the more the state restrains grain prices the more peasants' enthusiasm for growing grain will be dampened, which will finally lead to a shortage of grain resources.

It must be guaranteed that the major channels control the necessary grain resources for military grain and grain for special uses, such as grain stored against disasters and for restraining prices. Social stability can be guaranteed if the state stores enough grain for such purposes.

The existing state grain sectors should thoroughly separate the business, organizations and personnel of policy-related businesses from those involved in commercial operations. The policy-related businesses should include controlling grain resources, regulating operations and stabilizing the market. These businesses should stress creating economic returns benefiting society as a whole rather than solely seeking profits. The expenses of purchase and marketing, storage fees, interest and transportation fees should be paid by the financial departments of the government. Certain types of support and preferential treatment must be granted to ensure adequate floating capital and storage facilities. In addition, it should be made clear that each province and municipality must guarantee policy-related grain resources, and most warehouses should be set up in grain marketing areas.

The control of the grain market should be lifted. Grain resources controlled by major channels are main economic means adopted by the government to regulate and control the market. The grain market can be stabilized by collecting and storing grain when it is in abundant supply and selling it during times of shortage.

In addition, the grain risk fund system should be perfected. This is an indispensable condition for the successful marketizing of the grain purchasing and selling system. Efforts should be made to allocate in an appropriate manner the central and provincial grain risk funds as soon as possible, and the use of the funds should be strictly specified so as to promote the steady growth of grain production and maintain normal grain circulation order.

(VIII) Promoting Market Competition in the State-Owned Grain Sector

The policy-related aspect of grain should be thoroughly separated from its operation aspect, and the state-owned grain sector should be completely transformed into a group of operation enterprises.

The state-owned grain sector is the state's main channel for regulating grain supply and consumption, and the government grants it policy-related regulation and control functions. Meanwhile, it has operational functions as well as independent interests. The integration of policy-related functions with operational functions makes it hard to avoid using its monopoly position to make up losses from profits. In this way, the policy-related functions will inevitably be distorted and the state's regulation and control objectives can not be realized. Therefore, to guarantee the latter we should remove the policy-related functions from the state-owned grain sector and turn it into a series of enterprises specially engaged in handling agricultural products and assuming sole responsibility for their profits or losses. Enterprises which suffer from serious losses and can not make up the deficits within a short period of time may be allowed to go bankrupt, be auctioned or be annexed. As for small enterprises in difficulties, if they are state-owned they may be operated by non-governmental organizations. Leasing and contracting are also possible alternatives. Most circulation enterprises should adopt the enterprise system and be transformed into limited-liability companies or joint-stock companies. Meanwhile, their enterprise structure should be readjusted and enterprise groups should be organized so as to achieve economies of scale.

We should appropriately guide non-state-owned enterprises

into the grain market and allow multi-level grain business. As to the marketization of grain, the state-owned grain sector should no longer have a monopoly position. We should break down regional and trade boundaries, cultivate various intermediate organizations linking farm households with the market and carry out multi-channel competitive operations.

(IX) Solving the Long-Standing Problem of Grain Supply with Scientific Research as the Core

In the past two years the market prices of grain have gone up and down sharply. This has been caused by government interference rather than by problems in grain production. In the immediate future, so long as a national unified grain market is set up different localities may complement each other in terms of grain, and the fluctuation of market prices will be on a smaller scale. Though China will not have a problem of grain production in the near future, the situation in grain production is gloomy in the long term. Since the founding of New China in 1949 the country's total grain output has increased by 2.8 times. However, in the same period the population has doubled. Therefore, grain for per capita has increased by nearly one third. China's population, now increasing at a rate of 15 million people a year, will continue to increase in the coming decades. Along with the population growth, the demand for grain will also increase, but thanks to the rapid rise of national per capita income the demand for grain will decline, while the demand for refined foodstuffs and forage grain will rise sharply. However, the expansion of foodstuff and forage processing will call for more grain to be supplied. It is not realistic for China, a country with a population of 1.2 billion, to import a large amount of grain to satisfy its increasing domestic demand.

In general, there are two ways to increase total grain output: First, by expanding grain growing areas, and second, by raising the per-*mu* yield. Since 1957 China's cultivated areas have shrunk year by year. In 1994 China lost 5.969 million *mu* of cultivated land. Even if all localities, under the guidance of the government, make efforts to protect cultivated areas, the reduction of cultivated areas can only be slow down. Moreover, along with the

CHAPTER III MARKETIZATION OF PURCHASE AND SALES SYSTEMS

economic development, it is unavoidable that cash crops will occupy more and more grain growing areas. Hence to increase per-*mu* yield is the only way for China to raise its total grain output in the future. In fact, since 1952 the increase of China's total grain output has been attributed to the rise in per-*mu* yield. Therefore, the long-term grain policies should be centered on the increase of per-*mu* yield.

China's agriculture is well known for intensive cultivation, and the per-*mu* yield has always been high, especially since 1979, when the reform of the rural economy marked by the contract responsibility system based on the household and with remuneration linked to output was carried out. In 1990 China's per-*mu* yield was 54 percent higher than the world's average level, and the per-*mu* yield of rice, which occupies a specially important position, was very close to the highest figure in the world. However, the China Agricultural Science Research Priorities, drawn up by a team which investigated 383 prefectures and cities and 400-plus agricultural research institutes between 1991 and 1993, states that in spite of China's per-*mu* yield being among the best in the world, there is still huge potential for increasing the per-*mu* yield of the major grain crops—equivalent to 3-4 times the current per-*mu* yield. It is commonly believed that if the grain growth rate can be raised to only one percent higher than the population growth rate in the corresponding period, it will be a great achievement.

But due to many technical and social restrictive factors, the potential of grain crops' per-*mu* yield can not be tapped. Only by overcoming these restrictive factors one by one will it be possible to raise actual per-*mu* yield of grain crops. The research findings contained in the China Agricultural Scientific Research Priorities indicate that crop characteristics will not be changed unless new varieties are cultivated. The restrictive factors, such as geography, environment, soil, climate, plant diseases and insect pests, can be alleviated through strengthening irrigation, and applying chemical fertilizers and pesticides. However, as China's current material input level is high, any further increase in costs will bring about only small economic returns. If grain prices on the market do not grow by a large margin the farmers, with the single household as the economic unit and having autonomy over production, will have no enthusiasm for increasing investment in grain production. However, new varieties of grain crops with strong adaptability, resistance and endurance, developed through agricultural research, promise low costs and good economic returns.

(X) Perfecting Macro Control of Grain

In 1994 some problems cropped up in purchasing and marketing grain as follows: First, some localities did not implement the State Council's specification that negotiated grain prices should be fixed according to demand, and price changes should be dictated by the market. Second, some places violated the State Council's order to lower local grain prices; they closed grain markets and exercised regional isolation. Third, some state-owned grain sectors sought exorbitant profits by purchasing grain by order at low prices and selling it at high prices.

The implementation of the "provincial governor responsibility system" is favorable to the founding of the national unified grain market. Since 1995, each provincial government has been responsible for the local grain production, purchase and marketing, circulation between provinces, market management, storage and regulation, i.e., the "provincial governor's responsibility system." It is an important measure in reforming China's state monopoly of purchase and marketing grain. As compared with the situation in which the central government provided the people all over the country with food, it is no doubt an important progress. To implement this system is aimed at that each locality should realize grain circulation between regions and the balance between supply and demand through making full use of the market rather than conduct isolated self-sufficient. It must be avoid reducing main producers' grain output, transferring more grain for other uses and conducting regional isolation.

The government's control over grain should be transferred from relying on the existing grain handling mechanism to re-establishing the government grain storage and regulation system.

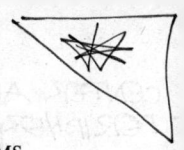

CHAPTER III MARKETIZATION OF PURCHASE AND SALES SYSTEMS

The state-owned grain sector and its branches will be split up into enterprises in the course of the reform, with their own independent interests. Therefore, the state should re-establish the grain storage and regulation system directly under the State Council, specializing in exercising policy-related regulatory functions.

Meanwhile, we should attach importance to the unbalanced variety structure in the supply of grain and the increase in the production and supply of rice.

A major cause of the sharp rise of grain prices in 1994 was the reduction of rice output, which led to an unbalanced variety structure of grain supplies. As compared with 1984, in 1994 China's population had increased by 15 percent, while rice output had declined by 0.9 percent. A sharp rise of grain prices starting at the end of 1993 was caused by the decrease of grain output. Therefore, planned guidance and economic policy means had to be adopted to increase China's rice output. In the meantime, we should make use of the international market to regulate the grain supply and demand domestically.

We should also make more use of the government's stored grain to restrain market prices. In the past, the prices of grain purchased by the government were often lower than the market prices. Hence the government found it difficult to purchase good-quality grain. So it is obvious that only by offering the market price or higher can the government purchase quality grain. In addition, only if the government improves its grain storage facilities and shortens the storage period, can stored grain regulate the market supply and demand and keep grain prices from going up.

III. The Construction of the Market System and the Founding of the National Unified Market

(I) The Founding of the National Unified Market Is Conducive to Stabilizing the Prices of Agricultural and Sideline Products and to Narrowing the Differences Among Regions

CENTER AND
PERIPHERY

THE REFORM AND DEVELOPMENT OF CHINA'S RURAL ECONOMY

In accordance with the theory of "balanced prices of key elements" in economics, if regions can trade their products on their own, not counting the costs of transportation and storage, the payment for various key elements will inevitably be equal. In other words, all laborers, no matter whether they are workers or peasants, and no matter whether they work in east China or west China, will get equal pay. Therefore, the more unified the market is, the smaller the differences among regions. Moreover, with a national unified large market, the industrial structure of each region will reflect its own comparative advantages. After a region's economy is developed, its comparative advantages as well as its industrial structure will undergo changes along with capital accumulation and the raising of wages. During this process the region will give up part of its market to other regions. Hence one region's development will promote the progress of other regions.

Take grain, for example. The provinces in east China have more people and less land than those in central China. Therefore, grain—which is a relatively intensive crop—has a comparative advantage in the provinces in central China. Along with the economic development and constant increase in the costs of land and labor in the provinces of east China, growing grain is becoming more and more uneconomical. But after the founding of the national unified market the provinces in east China with low economic returns from growing grain will gradually withdraw from the grain production field as their economies develop, and the demand for grain from the major producers in central China with comparatively high economic returns from grain production will increase. Grain prices will correspondingly rise, and farmers in the main grain-producing areas will obtain corresponding benefits. Moreover, so long as grain prices go up the farmers in the main grain growing areas will be more active in growing grain. In this way, the increased output from the main grain producers can make up for the reduced grain output of the areas with low economic returns from growing grain. This was shown by the grain production in 1993, at which time control was lifted from the prices and purchase and sales of vegetables, fruit, and fresh aquatic products. Therefore, so long as a large national

CHAPTER III MARKETIZATION OF PURCHASE AND SALES SYSTEMS

unified market is set up, the fluctuation of the market prices will be smaller than what it would be in a large number of small markets all over the country.

After the founding of a large national unified market, then eastern China will be more developed, and will need more resources from western China. This will mean that the income of farmers in western China will rise. So the development of east China will accelerate the economic growth of central and west China, and the income problems of central and western China can also be solved.

In addition, after the founding of a large national unified market, producers may directly contact buyers, and the government will no longer take the responsibility of providing urban citizens with grain and agricultural and sideline products at low prices, thus ridding itself of a heavy financial load. Moreover, as the products circulating via the market constantly grow in number the government's tax revenue will increase.

So far, a national unified market has not been formed. So it is unavoidable that the income differences between the farmers in central and western China and those in other regions are increasing. Therefore, to solve the farmers' income problems and regional income differences we must straighten out the macro policy environment, and set up a national unified market system to integrate the comparative advantages formed by the price system with the comparative advantages resulting from the resource structure.

Of course, it is impossible to completely eliminate the differences among regions and solve the problem of the low income of farmers. The solution to these problems also requires the founding of a national unified market of key elements, especially the setting up of a labor market. According to statistics, every year six million laborers from Sichuan Province work in other parts of China. If every laborer remits 1,000 yuan home every year, the total capital they remit to Sichuan will reach six billion yuan a year, more than the annual capital supplied by the central government to central and western China to develop township enterprises. Moreover, these laborers working in other places have brought technologies, market information and the experience of modernized production to their hometowns and have become fresh forces for the development of the market economy in central and western China. In addition, they play an important role in supporting the coastal areas of eastern China with labor and promoting the further economic development of eastern China.

(II) Integrating Trade, Industry and Agriculture and Guiding Peasants Toward the Market

Since the state lifted control from the sales of most agricultural products farmers' enthusiasm for developing production has been greatly mobilized. However, along with the development of the commodity economy, some deep contradictions in rural economic development have been exposed. The most prominent one is that the economy, production, processing and circulation in cities are divorced from those in the countryside. As a result, the following problems are manifest:

1. Production does not match circulation. Due to their traditional ties to the natural economy, China's farmers lack market information and the capacity to participate in market competition. So, more often than not, they turn out products blindly. They vie with each other to grow products which can be sold at high prices, with the result that supply soon exceeds demand, leading to periodic fluctuations. In addition, blind production causes havoc in circulation and processing.

2. The interest contradictions between urban and rural areas, and between industry, commerce and the farmers have sharpened.

At the beginning of the rural reform the state raised the purchasing prices of agricultural products by a comparatively large margin. Supplies of the major means of agricultural production were sufficient, their prices were stable and agriculture obtained fairly high economic returns. This was an important step contributing to the rapid development of agriculture. However, after 1985 the prices of means of agricultural production rose sharply, the comparative interests of agricultural production

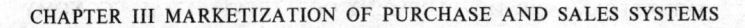

CHAPTER III MARKETIZATION OF PURCHASE AND SALES SYSTEMS

shrank and part of the farmers' benefits from the first step in the rural reform were lost. Meanwhile, the old system of cities developing separately from the countryside resulted in separating the processing of agricultural and sideline products from the processing industry. In this way, the farmers had to mainly rely on selling cheap raw materials rather than obtaining benefits from processing agricultural products, thus dampening their enthusiasm for developing agricultural production.

3. Small-scale and scattered production prevents the development of modernized agriculture. For instance, in general, rural households adopt traditional ways to raise 20-30 pigs, a dozen chickens or ducks and several dozen rabbits. Such a style of production suffers from low economic returns, long production periods, low-quality products and inability to produce in batches. The raising of domestic animals by rural households does not suit the demands of either international or domestic markets for large numbers and quick delivery of high-quality domestic animals. Thus, the traditional household method of raising livestock is unfavorable for the disposition of key production elements between urban and rural areas and between industries, to the bringing into play of urban and rural economic advantages as a whole, to the adoption of modernized equipment and the publicity of advanced science and technology. In a word, it militates against the modernization, specialization, socialization and commercialization of agriculture.

To solve the aforementioned contradictions, various forms of ownership have appeared along with the deepening of the rural reform and under the impetus of governments at different levels. In particular, enterprises which integrate trade, industry and agriculture, and produce, process and sell one or several kinds of products have shown strong vitality.

In accordance with the experiences of all localities, the basic way to develop the latter entities is as follows: <u>Taking into consideration the needs of the international and domestic markets</u>, regard the enterprises engaged in processing and selling agricultural and sideline products as the vanguard and household operation as the basis. Then, through socialized services and interest attractions, make agriculture, industry, commerce and trade form a common entity in which they share risks, interests and benefits. The basic methods are: Processing and business enterprises should go deep into the countryside, sign contracts with rural households in light of the market demand, set up production bases of agricultural and sideline products, provide necessary services, increase the resources of goods, organize processing and sell products on both domestic and international markets. Rural households should produce commodities in accordance with contracts and deliver ordered products on time. The economic and technical sectors should actively participate in offering services, and the administrative sector should handle macro control, coordination and instruction, so as to gradually form a new-type economic operation mechanism integrating production, processing and circulation under macro guidance.

There are various entities integrating trade, industry and agriculture into one and combining production, processing with marketing. Some are run by the national commerce departments, some by agricultural production departments, some by scientific and technical bodies and still others by specialized technical associations. They sell a wide variety of products, such as chickens, beef, milk cows, pigs, rabbits, aquatic products, fruit, tea and silkworm cocoons. The "dragon's head" enterprises have the following common characteristics: With sturdy economic and technological strength, they are free from the state's restrictions, they add extra value through processing, and have ready markets and high economic returns.

The entities that integrate trade, industry and agriculture and are engaged in production, processing and marketing mainly fall into the following types:

1. Those led by economically sound enterprises. Each focuses on producing, processing and marketing one kind of key product and integrating with the concerned departments and households to engage in operation.

2. Those guided by the market. These entities put stress on developing industries with particular advantages, perfecting the market system, widening commodity circulation channels, enlarg-

CHAPTER III MARKETIZATION OF PURCHASE AND SALES SYSTEMS

ing production scale by using the market guidance, and expanding operational setups, including processing, transporting and marketing.

3. Enterprise groups. By relying on advantages in the aspect of agricultural resources, they take agricultural production as the basis, industrial enterprises run by commerce as the head and comprehensive technical service as guarantee to form associated groups. Their basic functions are to connect with the market using the group's advantages, take risks together and link up with sources of fine-quality services and interests.

4. Entities whose operations are accelerated by science and technology. These are engaged in developing famous, quality, special and new products, and upgrading traditional products with new and high technologies so as to stimulate the development of production and processing, and open new markets. The trade-industry-agriculture entities formed on the basis of science and technology have a bright future in the market, and enjoy good economic returns and business vitality.

5. Associations and federations. Associations are founded to provide compensation and after-sales services, and supply technologies, improved varieties and means of production to farmers. They function to closely integrate production, science and technology with the market so as to increase economic returns and make farmers become better off together.

Integrated trade-industry-agriculture and production-processing-marketing operations are important means of deepening urban and rural reform and developing the rural economy. They are also good ways of guiding agriculture toward the market economy, and they effectively solve the contradictions between scattered rural operations and the unified market, and between traditional and modernized agriculture. They bring production and processing closer to circulation and effectively improve the intensification level of agriculture, strengthen the collectives' economic strength and help peasants become rich.

These entities help to combine urban reform with rural reform and accelerate the founding of new urban and rural economic relations. The deepening of urban and rural reform will

[handwritten note: THE SIGNBOARD: COUPLE IMAGINING THE HIGHRISES OF DENSE COMMUNITY]

THE REFORM AND DEVELOPMENT OF CHINA'S RURAL ECONOMY

eventually overcome the long-standing separation of cities from the countryside, production from marketing and agriculture from commerce.

As farmers' household operations fall into line with the demands of the unified market the transition from the self-supporting or semi-self-supporting economy to the commodity economy is realized. The trade-industry-agriculture and production-processing-marketing operations are linked with the domestic and international markets at one end and with millions of households at the other, thus closely integrating production, purchasing, processing, storage, transportation and marketing and solving the problem of the separation of production from the market.

The contradictions between small-scale operations and the adoption of scientific technologies will be solved and the transition from traditional agriculture to modern agriculture will be accomplished.

The new integrated operations system is conducive to the optimized allocation of key production elements, to realizing the complementary advantages between urban and rural areas, and among trade, industry and agriculture, and promoting the alliance of workers and peasants. Some places have taken the road of urban and rural areas helping each other for coordinated development and speeding the urbanization of the rural areas.

Intensified operations will be spurred and economies of scale will be realized. The trade-industry-agriculture and production-processing-marketing operations organize production in accordance with the demands of the domestic and international markets. To obtain stable and balanced supplies and ensure proper control, such operations need relatively large-scale concentrated production. As production difficulties are solved, rural households obtain more economic benefits through enlarging production scales on their own, breaking out of the limited sphere of household operation.

New control mechanisms can then arise, guaranteeing market supply and stabilizing market prices. When the trade-industry-agriculture and production-processing-marketing opera-

CHAPTER III MARKETIZATION OF PURCHASE AND SALES SYSTEMS

tions are adopted the government will be able to convey market information to the farmers in a timely fashion through core enterprises and guide production through eliminating blind production. Meanwhile, through a rational division of labor and management by contracts adopted by processing enterprises and operation departments, production and operation activities can be brought into the orbit of macro regulation and control.

The formation of such entities is also beneficial to increasing farmers' incomes and reinforcing the collectives' economic strength. Thanks to the adoption of improved varieties, the publicity of advanced technologies, the implementation of scientific management, the multi-level deep processing of products, and direct contacts between production enterprises and the market, output and economic profits have been increased and costs reduced, compared to when their incomes came from selling raw materials and primary products.

Changing the government's functions and setting up close ties between the Party and government departments and the people is accelerated by the adoption of the trade-industry-agriculture and production-processing-marketing operations, integrating all sectors through their common interests. The relations between processing enterprises, operation sectors and farmers are equal and mutually beneficial. Driven by common interests, processing enterprises and operation departments take the lead in providing good services to farmers, who in turn become enthusiastic about developing production.

(III) Developing the Commodities and Key Elements Markets, and Strengthening the Construction of Infrastructure Facilities and the Investment in Rural Education

There are two tasks which are urgent in the process of improving the commodities market. First, the various forms of state monopoly of purchase and marketing should be abolished. This because the state monopoly of purchase and marketing does not tally with the demands of founding a national integrated market system and is not a measure which can solve problems and create good conditions for deepening the reform; rather it sets up obstacles in this regard. Moreover, if the state monopoly of purchase and marketing is not abolished we will have no way to eliminate the problems in transregional circulation of agricultural products, and consequently, the growth of farmers' incomes will be hampered. Following the restoration of the state monopoly of purchase and marketing in 1994 the benefits of grain price restraint went to state-owned grain purchase and marketing sectors and grain sellers rather than the broad masses of urban residents with low incomes. Second, attention should be paid to problems in the production of grain and vegetables. If the regions with high incomes can basically supply themselves with agricultural products they do not need to purchase such products from the areas with low incomes. But the latter, while they get no income from selling agricultural products to the regions with high incomes, still need industrial products from the high-income areas, and this will inevitably lead to a worsening of income disparity between regions.

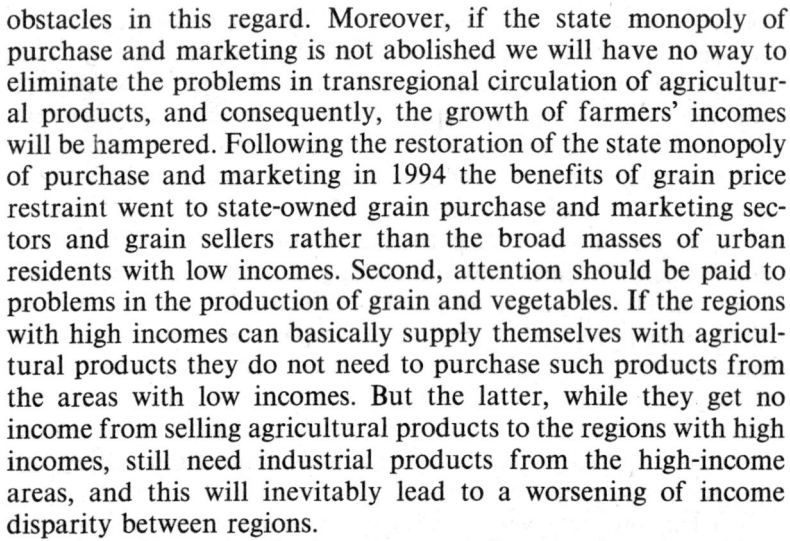

As to the market for key elements of production, three kinds of work need to be improved. First, the household registration system must be overhauled to meet the demand for a national unified labor market. The migration of surplus rural labor in recent years has resulted in increased incomes and pools of skill for their home areas. However, under the existing household registration system, migrant laborers may be driven back to their native places at any time. To stabilize the lives and production of such people we must reform the existing household registration system. But this does not mean that there will be uncontrolled migration from the countryside to the cities, as in other countries.

In addition, the government should strengthen the following work to form a national unified market:

1. Reinforce the construction of infrastructure facilities, such as storage, telecommunications and communications, and improve business conditions. At a certain price level, the lower the communications, transportation and storage costs, the larger the scope of the circulation of products, and the more benefits producers and consumers will obtain from the national unified market. The founding and perfection of communications, tele-

CHAPTER III MARKETIZATION OF PURCHASE AND SALES SYSTEMS

communications and financial facilities need large doses of investment and have obvious external effects. Nongovernmental organizations lack the ability and interest to invest in these aspects, especially in the early period of economic development. So the government should take the responsibility for such investment so that market development will not be hindered because of the shortage of these facilities.

2. Increase investment in rural education. As mentioned above, with the support of the national large unified market, if laborers have the same abilities their incomes should be the same. In light of this, the low incomes in the countryside are closely related to the low educational level there. Therefore, increasing investment in rural education is an important measure to narrow the differences in labor capital and income. Up to now, the educational conditions in rural areas have been much worse than those in cities. The main reason is that the educational expenses in cities are mainly borne by the government, and those in the countryside are mainly paid by the local people themselves. Hence, the government should first increase the investment in rural education, i.e., by reducing the costs of education in the countryside to create conditions for the farmers to improve themselves.

3. Strengthen financial backing for market growth. In theory, market development is an inevitable trend independent of the government's will. But this does not mean that the government may take a *laisser-faire* attitude. Exchange is the basis of the market. The exchange of products and key elements of production will only take place when the interests of buyer and seller coincide. The smaller the exchange risks, the larger the exchange's economic benefits will be, and the more active participants will become and the more brisk the market will be. Meanwhile, with the growth of the market, producers will be confronted with larger market risks, and so the government has the major responsibility for minimizing market exchange risks.

On the surface, commodity exchange means the transfer of commodities from one owner to the other owner, with payment flowing in the opposite direction to the commodities. However, in essence, the exchange of commodities is an exchange of ownership. Therefore, with clearly designated ownership, commodity exchange can progress smoothly. It is the government's duty to decide the ownership of various key elements and commodities by means of law and safeguard ownership so as to develop the market and promote the smooth circulation of commodities. To a large extent, market risks are caused by blind production and operation. With more information, enterprises can work out more appropriate policies and run smaller risks. Moreover, the change in consumer structure as well as in product demand may be forecast more accurately.

We should speed up market construction to provide agricultural and sideline products with exchange sites. In general, many agricultural products are still exchanged in their locales, so that the market's functions of information conveyance and regulation can hardly be brought into play. Therefore, we must further strengthen the construction of the rural market system to promote the circulation of rural commodities. Urban and rural markets are the sites where producers and consumers engage in exchange activities. Exchange fairs, which have flexibility, convenience and adaptability, should be encouraged.

The household registration system should be improved, and farmers should be encouraged to work and engage in business in small towns. The ownership of the land should be made clear, and the transfer of land with compensation should be allowed. Scientific and technical personnel should be encouraged to engage in technical contracting work in the countryside, popularize applied technologies and turn scientific and technological achievements into actual productivity. In short, we should promote the readjustment of the rural economic structure and raise the economic returns of the disposition of resources through founding and perfecting markets for key production elements.

We should improve the service system to help farmers enter the market. First of all, China should spare no effort to cultivate the market's intermediate organizations between farm households and the market. This is an effective way to establish close ties between scattered farm households with the daily-expanding mar-

CHAPTER III MARKETIZATION OF PURCHASE AND SALES SYSTEMS

ket. The following kinds of intermediate organizations are the key channels: First, the production-processing-marketing organizations headed by economic technological sectors. Some are headed by production sectors and others by operation or processing sectors. They separate some managerial and technical personnel from organs to set up economic and technical service entities. These entities link up with rural service organizations and specialized households to form agriculture-industry-commerce, and production-processing-marketing operations with commodity bases as the backing and services as ties, thus promoting the specialization and commercialization of production. Second, comprehensive service companies founded by townships and towns.

The purchase and marketing system for agricultural products should normalize the relations among production, supply and demand. Appropriate rewards and punishments should be adopted to guide and encourage farmers to implement their contracts, thus legalizing and normalizing the relations between the supply of and demand for agricultural products. We should organize and guide household operations to realize specialized production, integrated operation and socialized services. Production and operation should integrate crop planting, livestock raising and processing into one. At the same time, domestic and foreign trade, and trade, industry and commerce should be linked. The production and operation systems should be headed by the market, and the bases led by the market and linked with farm households.

We should coordinate services and macro control, and perfect the market economic system. First of all, we should strengthen the market legislation, and work out feasible market regulations so as to decide various behavior standards and penalty norms for the principal bodies in the market. At present, the main task is to perfect and implement business laws to guarantee that the various principal bodies publicly and equally participate in competition. Second, the industrial and commercial departments should correctly handle the relations between "relaxing" and "controlling," and should simplify procedures and provide services in terms of the examination and approval of industrial and commercial management. As to the verification of operation scope and methods, we should simplify procedures and provide services. The tax authorities should combine "flexibility" with "control." Financial departments should do their best to help the farmers who don't have enough capital to enter the market. Public security departments should ensure security in the countryside and in the market. Moreover, the relevant departments should regularly make public accurate information on the supply and demand situation of agricultural products, gradually set up a system of purchasing primary products by contract, stabilize the relations between production and marketing of primary products, and link up the various circulation channels. Operation and purchase units should sign purchase and marketing contracts on the premise of not letting farmers suffer losses, so as to mobilize their enthusiasm for developing production. Various means should be adopted to collect capital widely and gradually set up storage funds and price risk funds for the major agricultural products so as to regulate supply and demand on the market, stabilize market prices and protect producers' and consumers' interests. A state-collective-farmer agricultural investment system should be set up to increase the investment in agriculture.

(IV) Actively and Steadily Developing the Agricultural Products Futures Market

Though China's futures market for agricultural products has a short history it performs its basic function adequately.

First, futures prices for agricultural products have become the main reference for production and circulation enterprises. The Shanghai Grain and Edible Oil Commodity Exchange and the Zhengzhou Commodity Exchange play an important role in determining the futures prices of agricultural products and have attracted international attention.

Second, inflation-proof futures should be used to stabilize enterprise operations. In recent years some grass-roots grain units have started storing, purchasing and exchanging goods on commission to provide convenience to farmers. Enterprises put stored grain into circulation through the inflation-proof futures market.

CHAPTER III MARKETIZATION OF PURCHASE AND SALES SYSTEMS

Meanwhile, they purchase a certain number of futures contracts on the futures market to engage in opposite deals at appropriate prices, thus avoiding and dispersing the risks of price fluctuations after grain is sold.

Third, we should make use of the futures market to simplify circulation links. On the futures market, buyers and sellers do business directly at fairly competitive prices. Thanks to the reduction of many intermediate links, business costs decline.

Fourth, we should make use of the international futures trading business to promote the development of the import and export trade in agricultural products. Because of the rapid transmission of world futures trading information such as changes in commodity prices and exchange rates, the slow circulation period of Chinese agricultural products for foreign trade puts the agricultural industry at great risk. To reduce such risks, China's foreign trade enterprises have been engaged in futures value-protection business in the United States, Britain, Japan and Malaysia since the 1950s. Now the value of up to one-third to a half of China's wheat for export, and that of over half of its maize for export is protected through the Chicago Commodity Exchange. Soybeans amounting to as much as 500,000 tons are under value protection annually. The value protection of agricultural products for export has reduced operation risks and ensured the normal operation of export trade and purchase of agricultural products. The value protection of imported agricultural products have decreased costs for customers and ensured sufficient supplies. China imports 10 million tons of wheat or more, one million tons of sugar, and two million tons of edible oil from abroad every year, which all go through value protection on the international market.

Certain progress has been made in the expansion of China's futures market for agricultural products. However the market is still in the primary stage and on a trial basis. The following problems still exist:

First, at present, agricultural products on the market are mainly food grains other than wheat and rice and a small amount of raw materials for industry. The major agricultural products have not entered the market yet, and this affects futures functions in three ways: 1) Though control over the prices of sugar, edible oil and other daily necessities has been lifted and they are now regulated by the market, their prices have kept going up because of shrinking production. The futures trade in such products has been stopped by government order. 2) The production of daily necessities, such as rice and wheat, still can not fully meet the demand. To protect consumers' interests and maintain social stability, the "double-track system" of purchase and marketing of products is implemented and most products are regulated by the government rather than the market. The government was once prepared to allow such products to enter the futures market, but the plan was soon shelved. 3) Control over the marketing of important industrial raw materials, such as cotton under state monopoly of purchase and marketing, should not be restricted by futures contracts. In light of China's agricultural production and demand, the country does not have the material conditions for developing the agricultural product futures market in an all-round way. In addition, trade in small varieties of agricultural products has only just started.

Second, in China, due to scattered agricultural production, small operation scale and backward communications, the farmers do not have the timely information they need to participate in the futures market.

Third, business behavior has not been standardized, and the imperfect risk control system can not effectively mitigate trade risks. As the futures market is controlled by big enterprises, speculation runs rampant and its functions can not be brought into full play.

When working out measures for the development of China's futures market for agricultural products, the following should be taken into consideration:

First, within a certain period of time China should still adhere to the policy of making experiments steadily and promote the transition toward standardization. At the beginning, China's futures market for agricultural products lacked unified management and legislation. But during the experiments the futures

CHAPTER III MARKETIZATION OF PURCHASE AND SALES SYSTEMS

market got fully under way. However, the conditions are not yet fully mature. It is necessary to continue to make experiments steadily for a certain period of time.

Second, China needs to standardize the management system and legislation pertaining to the futures market for agricultural products. A three-tier system consisting of government supervision, self-management by trade associations and self-discipline is desirable for futures exchanges.

Third, China should optimize the structure of members and develop hedging. One of the reasons why speculation is widespread in China's futures market for agricultural products is the irrational structure of members, and another is that only a few members are engaged in hedging.

Fourth, membership is a standardized organizational form for stock and futures exchanges. But at present, various traditional and backward influences make it premature to institute the membership system for futures exchanges in China, so we can only make some experiments. For instance, the Shanghai Commodities Exchange implemented the membership system on a trial basis on January 1995.

Fifth, the authorities should strengthen control over brokerage companies, which are vital to the functioning of futures trading in agricultural products.

1. China should work out and promulgate laws and regulations on futures operation organs as soon as possible and realize the standardization of the management of brokerage companies. Brokerage companies that do business without licenses or do not conform to the requirements should have their operations suspended until the situation is rectified.

2. The capital of brokerage companies should be strictly supervised. A brokerage company must register its capital and deposit a certain proportion of the cash it collects from clients in the bank as a guarantee.

3. China should reinforce the management of double trade risks.

(V) Developing the Production of Vegetables in Accordance

THE REFORM AND DEVELOPMENT OF CHINA'S RURAL ECONOMY

with the Laws of the Market Economy

1. Vegetables are daily necessities, and governments at all levels should attach great importance to the adequate supply of vegetables. The premier himself is in charge of the production of vegetables. In addition, the State Council has an Office for the Management of the National Production of Vegetables. In each large and medium-sized city the mayor is responsible for the production of vegetables. Urban residents complain about the rapid rise of vegetable prices. However, the vegetable growers are not receiving extra benefits from the price rises. As to this question, public opinion is very strong, and the premier and mayors show great concern over it. Hence many measures have been adopted. But in light of the reality, the rise of vegetable prices on their own can not be easily controlled by administrative measures. Along with the development of China's market economy and weakened control of the prices of vegetables, the effects of government intervention are becoming less and less on the production, and wholesale and retail sales of vegetables.

2. The current state of the production and circulation of vegetables. In 1994 the vegetable growing areas in China totaled 126 million *mu*, equivalent to the total cultivated land of Guangdong, Guangxi and Fujian. In 1993 the total output of vegetables reached 210.6 billion kg. At present per capita consumption in cities is more than 150 kg annually. Of the expenditures per capita in cities, 50 percent goes on basic foodstuffs, 35 percent on non-staple foodstuffs and five percent on vegetables.

Along with the development of vegetable production, the traditional isolated production and supply on the spot has gradually be replaced by a more rational three-tier layout of vegetable resources, with permanent vegetable fields on the outskirts of cities as the first line of production, vegetable fields in the outer suburbs and in the neighboring counties as the second line of production, and the production bases for the transport of vegetables from the south to the north, and from the west to the east as the third line of production. In China the following setup has been formed: First, the five provinces and one autonomous region

CHAPTER III MARKETIZATION OF PURCHASE AND SALES SYSTEMS

in the south, i.e., Hainan, Guangdong, Guangxi, Fujian, Yunnan and Sichuan, are large natural hothouses. There the commodity vegetable areas exceed 400 *mu*. Every year vegetables transported from the south to the north greatly enrich the vegetable markets in north China. Second, the vegetable producers in the Yellow and Huaihe river valleys provide over 10 billion kg of various types of vegetables to every part of the country in spring and summer. Third, the Zhangjiakou area in Hebei Province, with 500,000 *mu* of vegetable fields, supplies large quantities of fresh vegetables to Beijing and Tianjin every autumn. In addition, Shandong and Hebei have eight million *mu* of land for growing Chinese cabbages. Thanks to the increase in new varieties and quantities of vegetables, the important position of Chinese cabbages has obviously declined for the citizens of north China in winter. Fourth, the Hexi corridor in northwest China is also a large vegetable producer. Moreover, in the past few years the output of vegetables in northeast China has also gone up greatly, and every year this region sends over 100 million kg of fresh vegetables to other parts of China.

China grows 209 varieties of vegetables. In addition, it imports varieties, develops new varieties and grows edible wild herbs. Each large and medium-sized city has also developed some special vegetables; their growing areas are expanding rapidly and their varieties are increasing. For instance, Beijing imports over 50 kinds of vegetable seeds from the south and abroad, such as celery, snow peas, lettuce and broccoli, which are no longer rarities to ordinary citizens.

3. The circulation of vegetables. In the past, the circulation and marketing of vegetables in cities were monopolized by state-owned vegetable companies and shops. They did not care about profits because they relied on large financial subsidies.

In the last 10 years, with the transition from the planned economy to the market economy, this state of situation has changed completely. State-owned vegetable companies and stores have collapsed and farmers have come to play the leading role in the urban vegetable wholesale and retail business. According to statistics, farmers handle 85 percent of the total vegetable business volume in Beijing, 80 percent in Tianjin and Shanghai and 75 percent in Guangzhou. It is probable that they handle about 80 percent of the vegetable business in most of China's other cities too.

4. Prices of vegetables. After the control of vegetable prices was lifted, these prices increased by 30 percent in three jumps, respectively in 1985, 1988 and 1994. The increase in vegetable prices in 1994 was nationwide, no matter whether a city had sufficient vegetables or not. Many people believe that the price rise in 1994 should be attributed to the gap between supply and demand. It was indeed a factor, but it was not the main one. The main reason was probably the sharp rise of the price level as a whole, i.e., because of inflation and currency devaluation. Along with the increase in residents' incomes, vegetable prices should be readjusted, and therefore, it is impossible for vegetable prices to fall.

In terms of price levels, according to the State Statistics Bureau's figures for 44 cities throughout the country in the first half of 1994, the average price per kg of ordinary vegetables was 1.98 yuan, and the average price per kg of fresh delicate vegetables was 2.28 yuan. In general, the retail sale prices of vegetables are about double the wholesale prices.

In conditions of a market economy seasonal variations in prices of vegetables are great.

5. Management stages for vegetables. In general, the reform of China's vegetable management system experienced the following four stages: The first stage was from the convening of the Third Plenary Session of the CPC's Tenth National Congress to the summer of 1984, when some large and medium-sized cities experimented with the system of farmers growing and selling vegetables on their own. This was the preparation stage for the reform. The second stage was from the summer of 1984 to the spring of 1988, the stage of combining flexible control with strict management. In July 1994 Wuhan took the lead in lifting control from the vegetable markets and their prices, thus breaking up the state monopoly of purchase and marketing vegetables which had lasted for 30-odd years. Many other large cities, such as Guang-

CHAPTER III MARKETIZATION OF PURCHASE AND SALES SYSTEMS

zhou and Xi'an, followed suit one after another, taking the road of combining flexible control with strict management. The third stage was from 1988 to 1992, when Premier Li Peng pointed out, "The fundamental way to solve the vegetable problem is to put our efforts into the reform." The basic orientation of the reform is to lift control, and mobilize peasants' enthusiasm for growing vegetables. The fourth stage was after the CPC 14th National Congress, since then the whole country has continued to deepen the reform and perfect the macro regulation and control system in light of the requirements for constructing the socialist market economy system.

6. Suggestions for boosting the production of vegetables. Small-scale production and circulation can not support the large national market, and the market monopoly held by small merchants and peddlers must be abolished. From the long-term point of view, there are two trends in vegetable circulation. First, the vegetable market is turning from being composed of local markets with each city as the center into a large national market. During this transition large vegetable bases are playing the core role. Products are sent to places throughout the country where the prices are high. Due to the improvement in transportation conditions and breakthroughs made in the technique of growing vegetables in sheds, the production of vegetables on the outskirts of cities is being replaced by agricultural production bases. In a few years the large areas of the Yellow and Huaihe river valleys will become the vegetable production centers for the cities in both south and north China. Second, high profits from the vegetable circulation field must accelerate the progress of circulation methods. At present, each large and medium-sized city shows great enthusiasm for the production of agricultural and sideline products. Shanghai and Beijing have also started experiments on setting up vegetable delivery centers and direct sales stores.

To meet the demands of economic development the adoption of the following measures may guarantee the further development of the production and circulation systems for vegetables.

First, to further expand the production of vegetables in the suburbs surrounding cities and large towns, we must adhere to the policy concerning vegetable production in these places "taking the suburbs as the main source of supply, and agricultural areas as the supplementary source, and subject to relevant regulations." In the past few years the use of vegetable fields for non-agricultural purposes has become serious. Meanwhile, the growth of economy in the outskirts has allowed the farmers to gain income from sources other than the growing and selling of vegetables. Therefore, the suburbs must resolutely preserve vegetable-growing areas on the one hand and change small-area production to effective large scale production on the other. Combining the production and marketing of vegetables, and reducing the intermediate links may greatly increase farmers' income from vegetable growing and maintain the steady supply of urban vegetables.

Second, a number of national vegetable production bases should be constructed, as well as centers for transporting vegetables from the south to the north, in Guangdong, Guangxi, Hainan and Sichuan provinces. Also, special production centers for winter and spring vegetables between the Yellow and Huaihe rivers and in north China for providing vegetables in the slack season should be built. As these areas are far from the markets, production must be in accord with the market demand. Only in this way can satisfactory economic benefits be obtained. At present, the countryside in these areas still practices small-scale, independent and blind production. More often than not, these areas have good products, but don't have good markets, in addition to unsound sales links, insufficient production quantity as a whole and great fluctuations in prices.

Third, we must take the raising of output and the improvement of quality as the main tasks and strengthen scientific and technological work in vegetable production. Improvements are needed in the selection and cultivation of good varieties, cultivation and management technologies, treatment after vegetables are gathered, storage, processing, packaging and transportation. At present farmers engaged in production, processing, transportation and marketing have not been trained, and so there are discrepancies in quality. In addition, due to a shortage of advanced

CHAPTER III MARKETIZATION OF PURCHASE AND SALES SYSTEMS

technologies and technical methods, large amounts of vegetables are lost during transportation and storage.

Fourth, agricultural industrialization must be realized through the construction of wholesale markets and the integration of production, processing and marketing operations. Farmers should be trained in the proper methods of producing, processing, transporting and marketing vegetables. The market network should be rapidly connected with each operation organization through the construction of a national wholesale market. Meanwhile, a group of large primary processing enterprises for making frozen and dehydrated vegetables should be set up. In this way, processed vegetables can enter the market directly and farmers' incomes may increase by a large margin due to the reduction of intermediate losses.

Fifth, intermediate costs can also be cut by mobilizing all pertinent enterprises, especially those with transportation means, to participate in the production and circulation of vegetables, and setting up flexible organizations to effectively combine the achievements of large production with the large market so as to benefit both producers and consumers.

Sixth, government subsidies and low-interest loans should be made available for key projects to reinforce operational strength. In light of the demands of the market economy, China should mainly invest capital in large-scale production, transportation and marketing entities in the suburbs, as well as in national production bases, to bolster the activities of production-processing-marketing entities.

The circulation of raw and fresh agricultural products should be organized, with the wholesale market as the center.

(1) Speeding up the reform of the agricultural product circulation system.

Most agricultural product wholesale markets in China were formed naturally in localities, and only a small number were set up according to plans. In these markets customers may order goods in accordance with samples. Experience shows that such wholesale markets assist both farmers and purchase and marketing organizations to enter the market, organize multi-channel commodity collection and distribution centers and boost transregional circulation. Thus they help to link large numbers of producers and consumers and promote the formation of a unified national market. They are located in wholesale links and hubs of commodity circulation as well as the centers of prices, information and services. In addition, as they are concentrated, they can be easily regulated, controlled and managed.

(2) On the basis of a systematic investigation of the current situation, experiences and problems of China's wholesale markets for agricultural products, we should work out policies that accord with the actual situation in China and are favorable to the development of wholesale market operations. In this regard it behoves us to study international experience, while taking into account the concrete situations of agricultural production, urban consumption, level of organization and circulation conditions in China.

(3) The government should put a certain amount of investment into the construction of public infrastructure facilities supporting wholesale markets.

(4) Large wholesale markets should play the leading role in the handling of certain kinds of agricultural products and integrated information networks should be set up so that accurate market forecasts can provide farmers and commerce operators with timely information on production and circulation.

(5) China should start to work out a law governing the operation of the wholesale market for agricultural products. The government's role in the wholesale market is focused on macro regulation, the installation of public infrastructure facilities, market exchange order, etc. At present, the most important task is to work out regulations on protecting agricultural business operators' rights and interests, equal competition and fair business order. Phenomena such as infringement upon the interests of parties concerned, including farmers and businessmen, administrative interference and monopolies should be stamped out.

(6) The government should help farmers to enter the circulation field, and try to improve the position of farmers in the market.

Chapter IV
Migration of Surplus Rural Labor and Urbanization of Rural Areas

I. Migration of Surplus Rural Labor During the Economic Restructuring

(I) Migration of Surplus Rural Labor Brings About Social Challenges

The migration of surplus rural labor is another acute problem that confronts the Chinese economy during the shift from the planned economy to the market economy. The harsh real fundamental problems are insufficient land, large population and high unemployment rate in the rural areas. It is estimated that China has 100-120 million surplus rural laborers, with a net growth of about 6-7 million every year.

Farmers now earn more money than before, and their increasing purchasing power is directly affecting the domestic market. But we must not underestimate the importance of the control of inflation. In some places many factories are operating under capacity. Inefficiency is one cause of the problem, and sluggish growth of farmers' incomes is the other, resulting in insufficient demand on the domestic market. If we ignore either of these factors we will have to face both inflation and economic stagnation. In this situation we must attach great importance to the migration of surplus rural laborers and continuous growth of farmers' incomes, for they have a deep influence on the economy as a whole.

The large-scale migration of surplus rural laborers is a serious social challenge. Among a host of economic problems there are two key ones. One is that the rapid growth of non-agricultural employment may cause a sudden increase of opportunity cost, thus inducing the prime cost of agricultural products to rise. The other is how the structure of the national economy, especially structure of production and distribution of the urban and rural economies, should be changed so as to absorb the huge numbers of surplus rural laborers. This migration is an outcome of the unbalanced development of different areas. Most surplus rural labor flows from agriculture to non-agricultural economic sectors, and from country to town and from underdeveloped areas to developed ones. There is no conclusion yet as to how this will influence the income differences among different regions. But there is no doubt that it causes problems with census registration, security, urban health and hygiene, family planning, education and other social aspects.

(II) Migration of Surplus Labor Brings About Changes in Rural Development and in the Farmers Themselves

Migration from the countryside plays a positive role in five respects: 1. It encourages the development of the rural market economy. The labor force engaging in the market economy swells and invigorates the sectors of production and circulation, thereby producing more commodities and getting them to the market. Moreover the growth of the labor market promotes the development of other key element markets. 2. It promotes agricultural modernization by creating favorable conditions for operating land on a large scale, realizing mechanization of farm work, and raising labor productivity and agricultural economic efficiency. 3. It promotes industrialization of the rural areas. The migration of rural laborers encourages the development of a diversified rural economy, non-agricultural trades and rural industry. 4. It stimulates the construction of small cities and towns, thus promoting urbanization. Urbanization is promoted in two ways: some rural laborers move to small cities and towns and help them to develop; others go to large- and medium-sized cities, boosting their populations. 5. It diversifies the sources of income for rural people, helping them to become well off.

In terms of accepted economic theory, the rural labor force

CHAPTER IV MIGRATION OF SURPLUS RURAL LABOR

should first flow from traditional, crude agriculture to modern, intensive agronomy. It is estimated that agriculture in China needs 200 million laborers if intensive farming is to be developed properly, and the best place for the surplus rural labor force is the secondary and service industries in the rural areas, i.e., township enterprises. At present, there are 123.453 million township enterprise employees, and an average of 6.34 million were absorbed annually in the past 15 years. However, in spite of the expansion of the township economy its capacity to absorb labor does not increase as rapidly as investment in fixed assets and output value do. In 1978 fixed assets per capita in township enterprises were valued at 812.28 yuan, and the output value per capita was 1,744.5 yuan. In 1993 these figures rose to 4,180.49 yuan and 25,584.75 yuan, respectively. By the end of this century there will be 170 million people working in township enterprises. In addition, some rural laborers flow to cities and towns to work in non-agricultural economic sectors. It is not clear how many of such people there are, but the estimated number is 10 million. In terms of region, most surplus rural laborers do not move far, working in township enterprises or near small towns. Some (about 35 million) have moved farther but remain within their own provinces, and others (25 million) go to other provinces or autonomous regions, where they find employment in both towns and the countryside. From inland areas to eastern and southern coastal areas of China is the main direction of the labor force migration. Sichuan and Anhui have the biggest numbers of rural laborers who have moved away, about six million and five million, respectively. Guangdong as a coastal province accepts the most rural laborers, about 7 million. Hainan also has much labor force from other provinces. In recent years, more and more people began to go to Jiangsu and Shanghai to work. In the meantime, there are also some workers with special skills who migrate from eastern to western areas to work in township enterprises or engage in border trade.

Considering both the large rural population and the limited resources, we conclude that the rural areas can not cope with the large numbers of surplus laborers, so about 100-150 million rural laborers have to leave—most of them for small cities and towns, and the rest for medium-sized and big cities. But since big cities are already very populous, the absorption of rural laborers should be restricted to the numbers necessary for urban construction.

There are two groups of migratory rural laborers. One sets down roots in township enterprises, and the other is constantly mobile between large and medium-sized cities, only occasionally settling down. This group tends to erode the traditional relationship between town and country.

The migration of rural labor makes great contributions to economic development and China's reform and opening up to the outside world.

1. Rural labor has brought about an economic boom in the developed areas and cities since the introduction of the policies of reform and opening up to the outside world. According to statistics, most of the top 500 township enterprises are located in advanced coastal areas, and 60 percent of their employees are rural workers from other parts of the country. About 80 percent of the rural laborers who work in Guangdong Province are clustered in the Zhujiang Delta, and 70 percent of them work in township enterprises. Wuxi County in Jiangsu Province has 130,000 workers from other parts of the country, accounting for one fourth of the non-agricultural laborers in the county. The reason why foreign businessmen are keen to invest in China is the inexpensive labor force, of which the floating rural labor force is an important component.

Now such workers can be found in just about every sector of the urban economy. In Beijing, Shanghai and other cities most vegetable growers, wholesalers and retailers are peasant workers. They also work running clothing stalls and repair shops, and are employed in restaurants, hotels, hospitals, government buildings and even in people's homes, serving as peddlers, shop assistants, street cleaners, guards and housekeepers. Every year they provide the government with quite a large amount in taxes. In Beijing there are 300,000 building workers from other parts of the country. Peasant workers can be found at all construction and mining sites. They also work on roads, railways and bridges.

CHAPTER IV MIGRATION OF SURPLUS RURAL LABOR

2. The migration of rural labor alleviates the employment pressure in underdeveloped areas and enables farmers to acquire wealth quickly. In some regions the number of farmers leaving home matches that of those working in local township enterprises.

3. Working away from home broadens the outlook of rural laborers and they acquire new skills, which they mostly take back with them to their home regions. Most of the returnees do not resume farm work but run township or private enterprises. In the central and western areas shortages of skills, capital and market information hinder the development of township enterprises. However, these are the very things that the returness can provide.

4. The migration of rural labor promotes the establishment and development of China's labor market, which is essential to the construction of a market economy. As farmers leave home to look for job opportunities in other parts of the country, they choose where to work, and enterprises choose whom to employ. Both sides decide independently without interference from administrative bodies, and the right to distribute labor power shifts from administrative departments to the labor market. Under these circumstances, a series of reforms will be carried out in the fields of employment, wages, training, etc. Now we can declare that without any state financial allocation, 60 million rural laborers have been employed through the market mechanism and a free flow of rural labor is in place.

(III) Erasing Prejudice and Getting a Correct Understanding of Rural Labor Migration

There are many different attitudes toward the migration of rural labor, producing different policies. The situation was the same with township enterprises in the 1980s. Prejudice against them led to three waves of restriction. Nevertheless, they survived and developed, proving their importance by their achievements. Now criticism has died out, their great contributions are widely recognized and support comes from all sectors of society.

Now it is the turn of migrant rural laborers. Criticism is mostly directed at laborers who move to other provinces, especially to medium-sized and large cities. People used to worry that they would cause social problems in the aspects of law and order, the family planning policy, etc. But while such concerns have some basis in fact, there is a growing acceptance of the migrant population.

At the same time, some people worry that agriculture will suffer if the younger, better-educated and more-skilled laborers join the "labor rush." But they are misled. Agriculture is not developed by accumulation of labor power. Considering China's cultivated area and the tools we use, only one third to a half of the current rural laborers are needed. It is a great waste to have all of them working in the fields. Surplus rural laborers who go to work in other places earn money which mostly flows back to their native regions.

Some people regard migrant rural labor as a dangerous phenomenon. They point out that through ages all the peasant uprisings which overthrew ruling dynasties in China were launched during migrations of peasants. In the past, the state bound peasants to the land, which resulted in a peaceful society. Today they have been set free, and could cause social upheavals. But the truth is that in Chinese history peasant uprisings were caused by the merciless exploitation of the common people by the ruling class. Today things are different. When peasants were bound to the land, our society was calm but rigid. After reform and opening up to the outside world the farmers were freed from the fields. Problems occurred, but the achievements were unprecedented. The new policies brought into play the initiative of the farmers, who pushed agricultural production to high-speed growth. Restructuring of the rural economy was carried out and township enterprises grew healthily. As a commodity economy developed in the countryside new small towns and cities appeared and more public facilities were constructed. Farmers' incomes increased rapidly, some farmers even becoming rich. All these achievements owe a great deal to the policy of allowing surplus rural labor to migrate freely.

It is also said that migrant farmers put an unacceptable burden on transportation, urban management and public order. There is some truth in this, but as long as controls are in place to

CHAPTER IV MIGRATION OF SURPLUS RURAL LABOR

prevent such people swamping cities, then great contributions can be made by migrant rural workers, especially as they take jobs that urban dwellers are unwilling to accept. As far as transportation is concerned, provinces such as Hubei, which have more migrant laborers than others, make special arrangements for travel during the Spring Festival and other holidays. So, by using measures such as increasing the numbers of buses and trains, this problem can be solved fairly easily.

Viewed from the angle of historical and social development, we must admit that this migration is positive. Cognizant of this fact, we should do our best to create more opportunities for migrant farmers.

Ignoring the historical trend and opposing, limiting and blocking this migration leads to social disorder and hinders the development of both the rural economy and society. But, understanding the demands of social development, supporting and guiding the migration, and trying to solve problems which occur all promote the vigorous development of the rural economy and society.

How to make full use of rural labor power and realize full employment in rural areas is a pressing problem in the development of the rural economy, and a problem of basic strategy concerning the overall situation of economic development and social progress. This problem becomes especially striking when the traditional planned economy is turning into a market economy.

Economic theory classifies labor power as a kind of resource. China, as a developing country with a large population, has rich rural labor resources. That is why, in the process of constructing socialism with Chinese characteristics, full employment and transformation of human resources into real productive forces are of specially great significance.

First, full employment of rural laborers is the objective requirement of reaching the "better-off level" of the rural people's livelihood. The major economic indices of the "better-off level" are the GNP and farmers' net income per capita. The increase of farmers' net income depends on the achievement of full employment, and since the 1980s it has been shown that this to a great extent depends on the migration of surplus rural labor. Second, full employment of rural labor is an intrinsic requirement for accelerating agricultural modernization. The important characteristics of agricultural modernization are mechanization and economies of scale. The key step in achieving economies of scale is to rationalize the distribution of factors of production, and this entails an appropriate reduction of the labor force. In microeconomics, if the efficiency of some of the factors of production in an business is promoted while the other factors remain stagnant, the overall efficiency will not be achieved. When idle labor leaves its original industry but is still jobless, invisible unemployment becomes visible, idle factors just shift from one field to another, and there is no progress in overall social efficiency. This hampers efforts to achieve economies of scale, the purpose of which is not only to free laborers from the land but to realize full employment, so that full use can be made of all factors of production and achieve the best economic benefits.

Third, the full employment of rural labor is a way to make the rural economy prosper and augment the overall strength of the country. The principal standards measuring the overall benefit of the national economy are utilization degree and ratio of resources. In the past, with the adoption of the strategy of giving priority to heavy industry and the policy of separating the cities from the countryside, China became more industrialized, but at the same time it became more divided. The rural labor force increased too rapidly to be absorbed by the levels of land and capital that the country's backward agriculture could provide. In this case, agriculture labor productivity almost stopped increasing, sometimes even decreased. This, for sure, limited rise of productivity of the whole national economy, though that in some industrial sections was high. That is why we had to create more job opportunities for the surplus rural labor force and why full employment is a prerequisite for raising both rural and national economic strength.

Fourth, full employment is the foundation of social stability

CHAPTER IV MIGRATION OF SURPLUS RURAL LABOR

in the countryside. Although labor as a factor of production can be replaced by other factors, it differs from other factors because of its unique characteristics. Other factors only cause financial losses if they are allowed to lie idle, but an idle labor force provokes social problems. If over a long period of time rural laborers can not give their full vigor to production, income per capita will definitely decrease, with living standards dropping accordingly. The more developed an area is, and the more rural labor it absorbs, the more social problems and disputes it has, and vice versa.

(IV) Comparative Advantage Provokes Chains of Migration

1. The comparative advantages of different sections of the national economy.

According to a survey carried out in 1993, the ratio of per capita income of urban residents compared to that of rural residents is 2.6:1. If we add all kinds of government subsidies and social welfare available to urban residents, and deduct the various fees from farmers' incomes, the ratio will become 5:1 or more. The income increase of urban compared to rural residents was in a ratio of 2:1 in 1981; that during 1983-84 was 1.7:1; in 1986 it was 1.95:1; in 1987 it was 2:1; in 1990 it was 2.2:1; and in 1993 it was 3.1:1. The average income of the 20 percent richest families in cities is more than ten times higher than that in rural areas. One of the reasons why there are income differences, and why they are becoming bigger is the scissors difference between the prices of farm and sideline products and that of means of agricultural production. For example, in 1992 the price index of farm and sideline products rose by 3.4 percent, while the retail price index of means of agricultural production went up by 7.3 percent. In 1993 the increase rates of the two indices were 12 percent and 16 percent, respectively. In recent years, as the prices of means of production have soared, farmers' incomes have plummeted. In 1994 the state raised the purchase prices of grain by an average of 30 percent, from 0.40 yuan to 0.52 yuan per *jin* (1 *jin* = 0.5 kg). But because of the rapidly increasing prices of means of agricultural production, the extra income accruing to farmers from selling grain at higher prices was just about enough to make up for the money they spent on the more expensive capital goods.

2. Regional comparative advantages.

For a long time the Chinese regional economy has developed in an unbalanced way. The economic gap among the eastern, central and western areas seems to be widening. The regional income difference is another basic reason for the migration of rural labor. During 1985-1991 the differential in per capita output value between the eastern and central regions increased from 452 yuan to 1,858 yuan. Between the eastern and western regions the gap was even wider. Farmers in the central and western areas are attracted by the affluence of the eastern regions, and flock there to earn higher incomes. This is a natural tendency when labor is allowed to flow freely.

Even in areas where township enterprises are developing well some farmers still leave for other parts of the country in search of higher incomes.

Under the completely planned economy, migration of rural laborers was limited. But since the implementation of the reform policy, farmers are no longer tied to the land, and in the process of establishing a market economy system, entailing the unification of urban and rural labor markets, they can move freely. At present, there are three forces pushing farmers from home: low income from agriculture, lack of non-agricultural employment opportunities at home and dissatisfaction with local social conditions.

Most migration is in the form of chain migration.

In China, as in other developing countries, there is an accelerated flow of peasants into the cities in the form of chain migration, i.e., newcomers not only get information from those who have arrived before them, they receive help in employment, lodgings and other aspects. At the end of a year, when these workers come home with bulging wallets and interesting news, they become heroes and the admiration of their fellow villagers. Since the export of labor services has become an important means of promoting the economy in underdeveloped areas, the local governments have begun to operate it as a profit-making industry.

CHPATER IV MIGRATION OF SURPLUS RURAL LABOR

Press reports and returning fellow villagers advertise the attractions of working away from home, attracting more and more people to join the exodus. After the Spring Festival holidays those who work in cities go back there, often taking other people with them. In this way, the phenomenon of chain migration takes place. In the big cities, chain migration results in the growth of areas where fellow provincials live in compact communities. For example, Nanjing has its "Henan Village" and "Anhui Village" and Beijing has its "Zhejiang Village." These types of community help to make migration to the cities more attractive to rural people.

The reasons for the existence of China's large rural labor force are many:

1. The surplus of rural labor is caused by the shrinkage of cultivated land and the increasing of the population. There is a limit to the amount of cultivated land, but theoretically there is no limit to the increase of population.

2. Because the productivity of agriculture is being raised, and less and less labor is needed for the same area of land. And the practice of the family contract system has brought the initiative of the farmers into full play. In addition, as the level of mechanization and electrification of agriculture is raised more farm land is brought under irrigation, and advanced agricultural techniques are spread. All these measures save labor and create a relative surplus rural labor force.

3. Due to the disparity in economic development between town and country, and the irrational structure of production within agriculture, there is a shortage of land for farmers to work on and not enough non-agricultural employment in the rural areas. Big and medium-sized cities balloon, while small towns develop only slowly and cannot absorb much extra labor. In this way, the process of urbanization is hampered. Meanwhile, the lopsided development of the structure of production and capital input into township industries impedes the growth of job opportunities for rural laborers.

4. Since farm work is seasonal, many farmers spend only two months a year working on the land, one month relaxing during

the Spring Festival, and the other nine months idle.

5. With the steady increase in population, the total number of laborers will increase year by year. But a bigger problem than the sheer numbers is the fact that farmers usually do not have the advanced skills or discipline demanded by modern industries.

Government policies as regards the migration of rural labor have to take into account certain characteristics of the rural population. First, due to the erroneous population policy adopted in the early years of the People's Republic, there was a rapid increase in the rural population in particular. In the 1950s, there were 170 million rural laborers. In 1978 there were 306.38 million, and by the year 2000 the number is estimated to rise to about 450 million. Currently the number of rural laborers is increasing by 15 million per year. Second, the Chinese rural population is poorly educated. Only 0.05 percent have college degrees, 8.8 percent graduated from high schools, 29.5 percent from junior middle schools, 40.7 percent from primary schools and 20.9 percent are illiterate. People with only primary school education and the illiterate account for 61.6 percent of all the rural laborers. In China, there are only four technicians per 10,000 laborers, whereas the number is 20 or more in developed countries.

The normal operations of a commodity economy require certain reserves of the factors of production. So there should also be reserves of labor power, as one of the factors of production. This means that there should always be some part of the labor force outside production and temporarily idle. This is to ensure the normal operation of the economy. For this reason, 100 percent employment is both impossible and against the law of economic development. The problem in China is that there are more surplus laborers than are needed as reserves. In the early years of capitalism in the advanced countries the situation was far different, as there was always a lack of labor.

But unlike other factors of production, laborers are consumers. They need food, clothing and housing no matter whether they are employed or idle.

In the Chinese countryside there are 80 million people living in poverty. In the poorest areas agriculture, merely crop cultivation, is the only means of employment. Usually these areas have a high birth rate, and the number of surplus laborers grows rapidly. The poorer an area is, the more unemployed laborers there are, and vice versa. Township enterprises not only provide job opportunities for local farmers, they also absorb rural laborers from more distant backward areas. Whether or not full employment is realized is the criterion for measuring how rich or poor a region is.

The three main reasons for large-scale migration of peasants from region to region are:

1. Historical reasons.

After the founding of New China in 1949 the country carried out the strategy of giving superiority to heavy industry. As a capital-intensive economic sector, heavy industry did not create many job opportunities at the beginning. Later, because state-owned enterprises did not make much profit and therefore had little capital accumulation, there were not enough positions in these enterprises for urban workers, let alone rural migrants. The state used administrative means to separate the country from the town, and capital accumulated from agriculture was transferred to cities for industrial development. Peasants were kept out of the cities and tied to the land, working with low efficiency. In the meantime, under "leftist" influence, diversified farming and rural industry were prohibited, which resulted in a unitary production structure. That is why the rural areas have for a long time stayed mired in poverty. The increasing population and shrinking cultivated land together create more and more unemployment among rural laborers, who spontaneously migrate to developed areas to seek work opportunities. In the late 1980s this migration became a virtual flood.

2. Present reasons.

Reform and opening up to the outside world brought economic recovery to China, and provided the conditions for the migration of rural laborers. (1) Coastal areas in east China and certain cities outpaced other parts of the country in economic development, and demand for labor grew rapidly there. These areas not only absorbed their own local rural labor, but also provided job opportunities for rural laborers from inland areas. (2) When the tension between demand for and supply of grain was eased and the new grain and oil purchase and sale system was implemented, it is easier for migratory peasants to buy grain and oil. Moreover, cities have abolished the rules that kept farmers out and begun to allow them to reside and work there. The market economy has finally freed farmers from the land and made it possible for them to migrate to other parts of the country to work according to market information. (3) Since the mid-1980s the economic gap between the central and western areas, which are underdeveloped, and the eastern areas, and that between country and town has been widening. Township enterprises in the central and western areas not only started later, but have developed more slowly. As a result, they are unable to offer enough job opportunities or satisfactory incomes.

3. Abnormal reasons.

Heavy financial burdens, declining comparative advantages of agriculture and interference by some government cadres are other causes of the streams of migrants from the land. Some local governments employ more workers than they can afford to pay, so they shift the financial burden onto the farmers through unreasonable apportioning of expenses and unreasonable fees. Second, wanton occupation of cultivated land, poor-quality seeds, chemical fertilizer and pesticides are other sources of complaint from farmers.

(V) The Migration of Rural Labor Is Getting Out of Control

The first step in reform in China's rural areas took families as the basic units of distribution of resources, instead of production teams. The family contract system appeared spontaneously among peasants before it was accepted as part of the official socio-economic system. This system for the first time allowed farmers to leave the land. In the past, farmers never took up any other occupation than farming; the rural people never left their native places except for further education, enlistment in the People's Liberation Army or marriage. But since the 1980s, when the contract system began to be carried out in an all-round way,

CHPATER IV MIGRATION OF SURPLUS RURAL LABOR

farmers have begun to leave the land in droves. Actually the migration of rural labor is the expression of the free disposition of labor. Some people have quit farming to work in factories or as peddlers, hoping to make more money. Since the rural population accounts for a large proportion of the country's total, such migration brings vitality to the whole of society, but at the same time it puts tremendous pressure on employment.

Families are more sensitive to benefit than production teams, so when they distribute resources they tend to seek the maximum benefit. At the beginning of the implementation of the household contract system, peasants were active in production because they then had their own land and hoped to make more profits out of it. Later, the hard-working farmers saw that those who had quit the land had generally done much better for themselves in terms of income. In fact, at the beginning of the reform income of the farmers increased rapidly, but the growth slowed down in the mid-1980s. According to statistics, during the period 1979-1984 the real annual net income per capita in rural areas went up by 15.1 percent; during the periods 1985-1988 and 1989-1991 the rates were five percent and 0.7 percent, respectively. The problem is that agriculture has not developed to the point at which it can develop economies of scale.

In recent years a phenomenon has appeared around the country which is worthy of notice. Cultivated land has been converted for use as orchards or fish ponds, basic farm land has been destroyed and the area of grain fields has decreased sharply. This random readjustment of the agricultural makeup will lead to a crisis, i.e., a drop in the output of grains and other essential agricultural products. The inherent disadvantage of the family contract system has now become apparent—decentralized farming becomes fragmented farming. In this form of farming, the use of farm land depends on how much return peasants can get from other industries, i.e., it depends on the comparative advantages of agriculture. If the comparative advantages of farm cultivation are high or incessantly increasing, both the cultivated land area and the proportion of cultivated land in all land for agricultural use will rise, and vice versa. Implementation of the contract system entitled peasants to decide for themselves how to use the land. But this, if it is taken to extremes, will entail a social cost which is higher than the benefits to individual households.

The new economic system in the rural areas has put more burdens on farmers, despite efforts by governments of all levels to lighten the load. Increases in the number of township cadres and management fees have raised the amount of township expenditure, and this causes a reduction in the amount of money for other uses. Meanwhile, heavy taxes are levied on grains and other agricultural products which produce little profit, or none at all, while land used for industry or the service trades, which make abundant profits, pay little tax.

If land is the umbilical cord which both supports and constrains Chinese farmers, a midwife is needed here to cut that umbilical cord and allow the farmers to live independent lives. The household contract system can not play this role because it keeps the tie between the farmers and the land. Even those who no longer do farm work have their own contracted land as an alternative source of income in case their other ventures fail. Also, they feel that they have a right to have their own land. If things go on like this, there will be three outcomes: The first one is that those who have steady non-farming jobs and high incomes will leave the land waste; the second is that those who do farm work in rural areas will not be able to expand their production scale; and the last one is that this not conducive to the development of the labor market. At present, the focus of the labor market is on the non-agricultural labor market in cities and towns, and multitudes of rural laborers are needed to develop this market. These laborers should be free to dispose of their labor, and this means that they should be free of all ties to the land. In this way they have no worries about their land when they are working away from home, and at the same time they have no alternative to being full-time workers.

It is estimated that the wave of migrant workers will continue to surge over the next ten years. During this period the main expression of population pressure will be the pressure of laborers' migration. The grounds for the above statement are as follows:

CHPATER IV MIGRATION OF SURPLUS RURAL LABOR

First, the number of new laborers in rural areas is increasing. During the period 1995-2000 the average annual increase will be 13 million. According to statistics, the proportion of labor power in the total population has gone up from 46.5 percent (1952) to 55.8 percent (1982) and 61.1 percent (1988). This trend will not change for the next 50 years.

Second, agricultural modernization and the achievement of economies of scale create more and more surplus laborers. It is estimated that in 2000 agricultural laborers will account for 45 percent of the total workers in China, and in 2010 the ratio may be as high as 30 percent—far more than either agriculture or township enterprises can absorb.

Third, peasants have become more aware of the advantages of migration, as this is encouraged by the media and certain industries.

The swelling tide of migrant labor mainly pounds at big and medium-sized cities, and may give rise to serious social problems in the near future. This is because 1. The establishment of the modern enterprise system and the social security system has turned invisible unemployment (the phenomenon of surplus employees) in the publicly-owned enterprises into visible unemployment. 2. Although new industries and technical advances create new job opportunities, farmers are seldom able to take advantage of them due to their limited skills. 3. Migrants bring poverty to the cities' suburbs, along with a certain amount of crime. In Guangzhou, Nanjing, Beijing and other big cities it has been shown that crime increases in proportion to the rise in the migrant population.

The movement of millions of peasants will for sure bring problems in the spheres of transportation, social security, family planning work and others. We should not regard all of them as flowing heedlessly into the cities, because in fact it is the market mechanism which draws them. During the Spring Festival holidays in 1989 a relevant department of the State Council interviewed 500 migrant rural workers who arrived at Beijing Railway Station. It found that 95.36 percent of them had learned of job opportunities from fellow villagers who had left home to work in cities before them. A report from the Ministry of Labor shows that 90 percent of migrant farmers have job targets. The autonomy of farmers in choosing jobs and of enterprises in employing workers is not likely to cause social chaos, especially since local governments have accumulated considerable experience in making proper arrangements for their movements and employment. Also, the law of supply and demand makes sure that surplus laborers do not go simply wherever they like. They have to consider where they are likely to find employment and if such employment will yield them more benefits than staying at home.

The transportation problem is an age-old one hindering the development of the national economy. Migrant farmers are not the cause of it, but a complicating factor. The best solution is not to prevent farmers moving, but to speed up transportation construction to increase capacity. Under the old planned economy farmers were confined to the land. It was a strange phenomenon that the majority of the Chinese population were seldom seen on trains. Now more and more peasants are traveling by train to seek work, and this seems reasonable. The shortage of rail carrying capacity can be overcome by such measures as those employed by the Ministry of Railways, which puts on extra trains around the Spring Festival holidays, the peak traveling time. The Chengdu Railway Bureau organizes rural laborers to leave Sichuan Province in advance of the holidays. In Wuhan extra wickets are opened to cater for the extra number of traveling rural workers.

As for the problem of public security, according to surveys conducted in Beijing, Suzhou and Wuxi, 99 percent of the migrant workers are law abiding. We should take into account that, away from home, these migrants do not get the same care from the government of their host communities as they get at home, and so it is no wonder that some of them get into trouble with the law, or, on the other hand, that their rights and interests are sometimes infringed upon. The solution to this problem has two aspects: On the one side, enterprises, relevant departments and street committees should make appropriate arrangements for the lives of the migrants in all aspects, including registration of residence, housing, food, membership credentials of the Communist Party and the Communist Youth League, and family planning. Only in this way, can these workers join normal and organized social activities, in which they receive education and supervision. On the other side, we should attach importance to the protection of their rights and interests.

(VI) Speeding Up the Comprehensive Development of Agriculture and Improving Its Labor Absorbability

Since the policies of reform and opening up were introduced standards of living have been steadily improving, and there is a growing demand for high-quality agricultural products both in variety and quantity. Such a big market provides an opportunity for adjustment of the agricultural makeup, development of agricultural products and more employment of rural laborers. In the process of restructuring the rural economy, we should put special stress on adjustments within agriculture, and following more favorable policies when providing capital and technologies. We should provide more aid for households developing diversified economies than to specialized households. <u>Families are the cells of a society. In China's rural areas a family is a unit of production, distribution and reproduction.</u> Many specific measures concerning the adjustment of the economic structure and distribution of labor are carried out by families. For this reason we must ensure that these policies and measures are spread to every household.

In underdeveloped areas most farm labor is devoted to growing crops. The more backward an area is, the more this is true. Previously we used to calculate that the grain supply decided how much of the labor force could leave the land. But due to the success of the reform of the rural economic system the amount of grain per capita soared, and when the supply was no longer a problem, rural laborers began to leave the land on a large scale. However, some regions then began to ignore agricultural production, especially crop cultivation. Blind construction of development areas and a real estate boom caused a sharp decrease in the area of cultivated land. In 1994 some 10 million *mu* of cultivated land were lost nationwide. Taking into consideration the four million *mu* of reclaimed wasteland, the net lost area of cultivated land was six million *mu*. Moreover, the low economic benefits of crop growing discouraged the farmers to the extent that they would either cultivate the land extensively or leave it idle. As a result, the grain yield fell sharply and the problem of grain supply became acute again.

II. The Development of Township Enterprises

(I) The Four-Stage Development of Township Enterprises

China's market-oriented reform began in the rural areas at the beginning of the 1980s. The continuing deepening of the economic reform, to a large degree, has depended on the rapid development of the rural economy, especially that of township enterprises. The contract household responsibility system made the first breach in the old planned economy, and the township enterprises made the second.

China's township enterprises are the inevitable result of the reform of the old planned economy and a necessary concomitant of the progress toward a market economy.

The development of township enterprises went through four stages:

The first covered the period from the start of the reform to 1984. In this period the household contract responsibility system invigorated the rural economy, the factors of production began to flow more smoothly and farmers started to engage in non-agricultural economic pursuits. The production team enterprises were renamed township enterprises, and the stage was set for rapid development.

The second period was from 1985 to 1988, when there were fluctuations in agricultural production. However, the township enterprises flourished, the rural economy enjoyed comprehensive development and farmers' incomes soared.

In 1984 the total grain yield had reached 400 million tons, or 400 kg per capita, which was close to the world average. This was

CHAPTER IV MIGRATION OF SURPLUS RURAL LABOR

considered to be the greatest achievement of the rural reform because it seemed that the food problem would soon be solved. However, the grain yield in 1985 saw a drop of 25 million tons, mainly due to the decreased profits from farm production. And the grain yield in the following three years did not break the record of 1984. This prompted calls for less support for township enterprises and more emphasis on grain production. But the development of township enterprises went full steam ahead, and their total output value was RMB 645.9 billion yuan in 1988, a more than sixfold increase over 1983's 101 billion yuan, with a nearly 40 percent increase rate per year. A total of 10 million surplus rural laborers were absorbed by these enterprises per year, and by 1988 they employed 95.45 million people, almost equal to the figure for workers in state-owned enterprises. Within a few years the total output value of township enterprises had exceeded that of agriculture and provided the main part of farmers' increased incomes. Although grain and cotton production fluctuated, the farmers still enjoyed an annual income increase rate of five percent. In the meantime, there was no obvious shortage of agricultural products in the cities. On the contrary, the supply of vegetables, fruits, aquatic products and animal by-products increased greatly.

From 1989 to 1991 was the third period, also an adjustment period. There was a credit squeeze and rural incomes stagnated, although agricultural production increased. Township enterprises confronted more difficulties.

Grain production started to climb again, due to a series of policies adopted over the years. The total grain yield in 1989 exceeded the record of 1984, and it continued to increase by an annual average of 4.6 percent in the following two years despite severe floods in 1991. However, farmers' incomes did not increase as much as expected because township enterprises were still undergoing difficulties and the price ratio between industrial and agricultural products was irrational. In 1989 farmers' incomes actually dropped 1.6 percent compared to the previous year, the first negative growth since the rural reform started. In 1990 there was a bumper harvest, but farmers' incomes only grew by 1.8

percent over the previous year, and in 1991 the figure was two percent. The average annual growth rate of these three years was only 0.7 percent. In consideration of the regional differences, the net income of the farmers in many regions saw decreases. Township enterprises enjoyed more freedom in developed coastal areas, especially in the Pearl River Delta. Being close to Hong Kong and Macao and the ancestral home of many overseas Chinese, the delta has introduced capital and techniques by means of processing with supplied materials, processing with supplied samples, assembling with supplied parts and compensation trade. Thus, a foreign-oriented economy has been developed and the former labor-intensive township enterprises have been transformed into technology-intensive and capital-intensive ones. The income of the farmers in the region increased at a faster pace than in the first two periods. In 1991 the total output value of township enterprises for the first time exceeded 1,000 billion yuan, reaching 1,100 billion yuan, including gross industrial output value of 850 billion yuan, one third of the nation's total industrial output value. Moreover, 31.9 percent of the net increase in the value of social products and 32 percent of per capita net income in the rural areas came from township enterprises.

The fourth period began with the publication of Deng Xiaoping's speech made during his southern China tour in early 1992. The reform and opening to the outside were accelerated, spurring the development of the foreign-oriented economy nationwide.

The value of exports from township enterprises had reached RMB 190 billion yuan by 1993, with the annual increase rate topping 60 percent for two years. In 1994 the figure was still growing. The number of newly established foreign-invested township enterprises has doubled and expanded from coastal areas to the inland and border provinces. The investment has come from not only Hong Kong, Macao and Taiwan but also European, North American and Southeast Asian countries, with increasing investment scale and larger projects. Township enterprises have become a promising new force in the national economy on a par with state-owned large and medium-sized enterprises.

CHAPTER IV MIGRATION OF SURPLUS RURAL LABOR

(II) Township Enterprises As the Driving Force of China's Market Economy

Why have township enterprises managed to overcome their difficulties one after another and developed at high speed while state-owned enterprises have failed to do so? The reason is that township enterprises were born in adverse circumstances, grew up amid difficulties and the whole process depended on the market mechanism rather than state plans.

Although township enterprises got off to a late start, were small in scale, and had poor equipment and a low level of technology from the very beginning, they had their own decision-making power and took full responsibility for their own profits and losses, which equipped them to participate in market competition. The fatal disadvantage of state-owned enterprises, despite all their superiorities over township enterprises, is that government administration departments intervened too much in their internal affairs. Since the beginning of the reform and opening to the outside world, the state-owned enterprises have a certain amount of autonomy in name but not in reality. In this sense, the rural people withstood the test of the market before the people of the urban areas.

Secondly, the products and technical structures of township enterprises enable them to exploit local advantages, that is, rich labor resources, while avoiding disadvantages, that is, insufficient capital. In the past, capital-intensive heavy industry was the first to be developed by mobilizing as many resources as possible under the central planning system. But heavy industry offered fewer employment chances and has a low capital turnover rate. Township enterprises mainly produce daily-use and light industrial products to meet the demands of the market. This kind of quick-circulation production is labor-intensive, requiring only a small amount of capital and a relatively low level of technology. In this way, township enterprises absorb a large number of surplus rural laborers and accumulate capital for the improvement of technology. Family- and individually-owned enterprises are flourishing in the Wenzhou area of Zhejiang Province, producing various kinds of daily necessities and have formed 15 specialized markets. Another example is the button market in Qiaotou Town, also in Zhejiang, the biggest button market in the Far East. This market handles 80 percent of the total sales of buttons in the nation.

Township enterprises are a product of the policies of reform and opening to the outside, and also of the non-planned economy which has grown up within the planned economy system. They will keep developing along with the deepening and widening of the reform. These enterprises buy raw materials and sell products on the market. As a result, non-planned prices have appeared. The development of township enterprises has promoted the flow and connections among factors of production, so the market has been playing increasingly important roles. The greatly improved economic efficiency and increased amount of resources, adding to the number of things outside the state plans, forced reform upon the mode of resources allocation and state economic policy. The original planned economy system had to co-exist with the market system and started to convert itself into a market economy. The township enterprises can develop according to their own conditions since they have the right to make their own decisions. Then the increase in the volume of products enlarges the volume of sales outside the state plans, and the expanded production needs the purchase of more raw materials outside the plans. Thus, the further development of unfettered township enterprises will exert a bigger impact on the planned sector until a new socialist market economy system emerges.

(III) The Development of Township Enterprises Absorbs Surplus Labor

So far, township enterprises have play the main role in absorbing the excessive rural labor force. At the same time, the farmers' willingness to invest in the non-agricultural sector and become rich has in turn promoted the development of township enterprises. Farmers, who had for a long period of time invested their limited savings in agriculture only and found themselves with little profit, turned to investing in these enterprises. It is

CHAPTER IV MIGRATION OF SURPLUS RURAL LABOR

estimated that an average of 20 percent of the income of rural people has come from township enterprises in recent years; in some areas with more developed township enterprises the figure is over 50 percent. China's rural industrialization has been accelerating since the 1980s. In 1987 for the first time the total agricultural output value accounted for below 50 percent of the total rural social output value. And in 1992 the total rural industrial output value for the first time accounted for over 50 percent of the total rural social output value, which is a sign of the takeoff of China's rural industrialization.

The leading index in China's rapid industrial growth is the increase rate of the number of township enterprises. Taking the 1978 figure as the base, the industrial output value of township enterprises has doubled every four years. Since the beginning of the 1990s the gap between the growth rates of urban industries and township industries has grown even wider. The industrial output value at the county level and above increased by 12.9 percent and 21.2 percent in 1991 and 1992, respectively, of which the industrial output value of township enterprises increased by 25 percent and 52.2 percent, respectively. The industrial output value of township enterprises accounted for 9.1 percent of the gross national industrial output value in 1978, 16.3 percent in 1984, 23.8 percent in 1989, 30.8 percent in 1991 and 36.8 percent in 1992.

The rapid growth of township enterprises has created many employment opportunities for surplus rural laborers. There have appeared two modes of rural industrialization—the collective mode and the individual mode—with southern Jiangsu Province and Wenzhou City as respective examples. The individual mode has played an important role in promoting the development of individual and privately-owned businesses. But it has the shortcomings of primitive accumulation and poor protection of the interests of employees. The collective mode was formed in the wake of the industrialization drive of rural communities, and some communities have remained strong in the process of initiating enterprises and other non-agricultural economic undertakings, such as those in Suzhou, Wuxi and Changzhou cities in southern Jiangsu Province.

The industrialization drive organized by rural communities originated in efforts to achieve the following targets—1) Creating employment opportunities for surplus laborers; 2) Increasing incomes to improve people's livelihoods; 3) Increasing the local finance income; and 4) Doubling the gross output value as soon as possible. The first and second targets are the same with every family, so industrialization is welcomed by all community members.

The role of the collective mode has always been confirmed and sometimes even exaggerated. But in fact it, too, has its drawbacks. Taking the township enterprises of Suzhou City as examples, there are the following problems: 1) Over-investment. More than 170 emulsion glove production lines set up in 1987 have suffered total losses of 300 million yuan. 2) Low accumulation level. The circulating fund of all township enterprises has lingered at about 10 percent. 3) Too many extra financial charges. More than 80 kinds of charges and "donations" demanded by organs of supervision account for over 50 percent of the annual profits of the enterprises. 4) Low cost-effectiveness. The average profit on every 100 yuan-worth of products is only two to three yuan, and the total return on capital is only about four percent. These problems are mainly due to the unclear property rights and the continued interference of government administration with enterprises.

(IV) Systematic Innovation of Township Enterprises

1. The keys to the development of township enterprises are the flexible operation mechanism and clear interests mechanism. As the main body of market activities, township enterprises on the one hand have improved the formation and development of the market, and on the other they themselves are motivated by the stimulation of the market mechanism. With this operation mechanism the enterprises have full management autonomy and are responsible for their own profits and losses, which reflect interest relations.

The mainstay of township enterprises is the independence of

CHAPTER IV MIGRATION OF SURPLUS RURAL LABOR

individual economic interests, ensuring that responsibility is taken for profits and losses. This independence must be safeguarded.

2. The joint-stock system is helpful for the clarification of property rights and the standardization of enterprise management.

Individual interests, in different forms, are clear in privately-owned or individually-owned enterprises. But they are not at all clear in the collectively-owned enterprises at the county and village levels. The advantages of the joint-stock system are:

First, property rights are made clear, and individual and collective interests are linked. During the pioneering period of every township enterprise, inexplicit individual interests do not hinder, and sometimes even help, the development of the enterprise. The problems arise when the enterprise has been developed to a certain stage or scale. Farmers in many places feel that there is little difference as far as taxes are concerned whether an enterprise is owned by a collective, an individual or a private body. The collective-owned enterprises seem as if they are owned by the village cadres. The people who work in them never know the income and expenses, and the fact that they are the owners of the enterprises is not made clear to them. Some cadres think that they themselves should have most of the management power, because they did the pioneering work in setting up the enterprises. And some even try to pass the management of the enterprises on to their offspring.

Second, management is standardized and the managerial skill level is raised. A share-holding enterprise usually has three levels in its managerial system. The first is the shareholders' meeting, the highest authority and the representative of the ultimate ownership of the enterprise. The second is the board of directors, which makes daily decisions and is composed of representatives of the enterprise's interest. The third is the director and manager of the enterprise, who, together with the other staff members, embodies the operational interest. Thus, the practice of the share-holding system, with the above checks and balances, may help standardize and demarcate management functions and spheres. For example, the financial system must be transparent and rational. Also, it may help the separation of ownership from management and raise the level of management.

Third, the system helps to accumulate capital to further develop township enterprises. Farmers are only willing to invest their savings in enterprises when the ownership has been clarified and the managerial level has been improved. With a flexible market mechanism, perfected managerial system and assured capital, in addition to inputs of skills and technology, the township enterprises are assured of rapid development.

The joint-stock system is one which can enable township enterprises to develop into modern enterprises.

The joint-stock system is a basic system directly related to the combination and flow of resources under market economy conditions, and is applicable to many industries and economic fields.

Moreover, the joint-stock system separates assets from value so to solve the contradiction between the forces of production and scattered assets. It is also able to cater to the needs of the owners of various factors of production (capital, land, factory buildings, equipment, labor and intellectual property rights) to participate in the establishment and development of enterprises. These owners will take part in the management of the enterprises and share both profits and risks. Such a combination of factors of production will play an important role in motivating the owners to participate in economic development.

The joint-stock system from the very beginning combines capital and labor standards, which are based on different principles, in microeconomic construction. This is conducive to the formation and development of microeconomic entities and will quicken the transition toward a market economy.

III. The Construction of Small Towns

(I) The Development of Small Towns Will Slow the Current Labor Migration

1. An absorption system with greater elasticity.

There are two major channels for the transfer of surplus

CHAPTER IV MIGRATION OF SURPLUS RURAL LABOR

rural labor—one is transfer to secondary and tertiary industries in the rural areas, and the other is transfer to the cities. The former channel developed earlier than the latter, but the cities are now absorbing surplus rural labor at a faster rate.

In view of China's actual situation, if hundreds of thousands of farmers poured into the cities, many problems would emerge, like overburdened transportation and a breakdown in social services. Moreover, the job market in the cities is almost saturated. What is more serious is that the job markets have been tight simultaneously in both the urban and rural areas since the beginning of the 1990s. The development of small towns in rural areas together with rural industrialization will not only lead to complete absorption of surplus rural labor but also optimize the allocation of resources in rural areas and narrow the gap between the cities and rural areas.

2. The small towns function as reservoirs of labor.

The development of rural industries instilled energy into agricultural production, which has only been limited by supply and demand. Meanwhile, it has greatly changed the situation of estrangement between the cities and the countryside and created important conditions for solving the problems facing urbanization and for the quickening of township system reform. Previously there had been an impassable chasm between town dweller and peasant in China, but in 1984 a document on peasants' residence in towns issued by the State Council bridged this gap for the first time. The document stipulated that the public security departments should issue residence permits to migrant rural laborers and their families so long as they have a fixed job or business and have a residence.

The gross output value of the 118 township enterprises in Shengze, a new town in Jiangsu Province, totaled 2.8 billion yuan in 1991 and the per capita output value reached 6,000 US dollars, which exceeds that of the Republic of Korea. Another example is Longgang Town in Zhejiang Province, which was an obscure village up to 1984. After only two years the local farmers had built it up into a town with 27 streets, nearly one million square meters of construction areas and a population of 30,000. This was done at a cost of 160 million yuan, only nine million yuan of which was provided by the state. By 1993 the town's population had grown to 130,000 and the annual output value to 800 million yuan.

The newly emerging small towns in rural areas are in response to the demand of rural industrial development and the foundation of rural social transformation. In China, the traditional function of small towns is to distribute agricultural and sideline products. But in the past ten years the small town has become a center of production, service, entertainment, education and information as well. Thus, the farmers no longer depend on large and medium-sized cities as much as before. The development of small towns will inevitably bring urban civilization to the rural areas and modernize the life style of the rural inhabitants.

The development of small towns is promoting the urbanization of rural areas and narrowing the gap between the urban and rural areas. However, people hold different opinions on the development of small towns. Some think that the disadvantages outweigh the advantages, while others see the new towns as ideal for soaking up surplus rural labor.

The best way to accelerate the urbanization of rural areas is to concentrate industries there. China's township and family enterprises are scattered among villages, and this entails many disadvantages, such as inconvenient transportation, slow access to information and waste of land resources. The central towns should be selected for the gathering of industries by improving their investment environments and adopting preferential policies to attract township and family enterprises. Another way is to open the small towns and let peasants settle down there through registration.

(II) Bringing the Potential of Small Towns to Absorb Rural Surplus Labor into Full Play

Currently there are 170 million surplus rural laborers in China, and by the end of the century this number will soar to over 200 million. The country's more than 19,000 small towns have absorbed more than 30 million surplus rural laborers over

CHAPTER IV MIGRATION OF SURPLUS RURAL LABOR

the past ten years, accounting for over 30 percent of such people. However, the current absorption capability of the small towns in China is only 1,600 surplus rural laborers each. If the capability were to be doubled, then 30 million more laborers could be absorbed.

Compared to large and medium-sized cities, the small towns have the following advantages with respect to absorbing rural surplus laborers:

First, there are more employment opportunities in small towns because they have small populations. The new industries have a large capacity for absorbing surplus rural laborers. Farmers with skills can engage in secondary and tertiary industries, and those who do not can work in primary industry.

The small towns' location between the cities and the countryside gives them features of both life styles, and so farmers find it easier to settle down there than in the big cities. They also find living expenses there less than in the big cities. This is especially so in the case of transportation if the farmers come from nearby areas.

Another advantage of small towns is that the migrants find information on job opportunities and pay levels more quickly there than in larger urban communities.

Finally, it is easier for farmers to set up businesses in small towns, where there is little entrenched competition and the capital requirement is less.

The big cities are actually taking steps to stem the influx of surplus rural labor. Currently there are 60 million rural laborers working away from home, most of them forming the floating populations of big cities. By the end of this century, a total of 200 million farmers will no longer engage in agriculture and will seek work elsewhere. It is inevitable that new towns will spring up to absorb them.

(III) Residence Permit Restrictions Should Be Relaxed and Land, Social and Capital Policies Should Be Beefed Up

The goal of residence permit system reform in the near future shall be the gradual relaxation of restrictions on the transfer of residence from the countryside to the towns. Surplus rural laborers who have steady jobs, incomes and places to live should be able to enjoy the same rights and duties as urbanites. The land policy must also be reformed. Land for construction should be strictly planned and developed in a unified way. Sales of land should take the forms of contract, bidding or auction, and land for different uses should be priced differently. Agricultural land should not be occupied at random.

(IV) Enlarging the Cities

The slow change of China's employment structure is closely related to the low rate of urbanization and the imperfect structure of the cities. Today China's urban population only accounts for 26 percent of the total. Most manufacturing industries are concentrated in the large and medium-sized cities, and the smaller cities do not yet play their corresponding role as locations of tertiary industry. The development of international and domestic markets, commercial goods markets and markets for factors of production requires that the proportion of cities be increased, with a few of them acting as international transfer centers and the others mainly engaging in manufacturing or tertiary industries. Only when the number of cities is increased appropriately and their functions are perfected will more competitive foreign-oriented enterprises appear. In the meantime, the present labor-intensive industries will be gradually transferred to backward areas. On this basis, the residence permit system can be reformed, the labor market developed and population transfer guided so as to better the lives of urban and rural residents and create new demand which will in turn promote economic development.

Now a development mode has been formed which centers on large and medium-sized cities such as Xiamen, Guangzhou, Shanghai, Beijing, Tianjin, Wuhan and Chongqing.

Chapter V
Changing the Functions of the Government and Coordinated Development in Rural Areas

I. Government Functions and Measures of Macro Control

(I) In the Conditions of a Market Economy It Is Still Necessary for the Government to Intervene in the Main Spheres of Agriculture

Government intervention in the development of market agriculture is different from the traditional planned management of agriculture. In the conditions of a market economy government intervention in the development of agriculture is mainly reflected in the setting up and perfection of the systems of information, storage, circulation, processing and support. It also reflects the necessity for government activity in the fields of financial and welfare policies and the legislation concerned in order to guarantee the continuous development of agriculture.

1. The spheres directly acted on by the government in the development of market agriculture are as follows:

Information system: Using information to guide agricultural production, eliminating blind production, and playing the government's due role in drawing up agricultural production plans.

The continual improvement of China's marketing system has been accompanied by profound changes in the sphere of agricultural macro management. The system of planned management of traditional agriculture has gradually disintegrated, with the result that the purchase and sale of agricultural and sideline products and plans for agricultural production have been completely decontrolled in the great majority of China's provinces and cities.

But the farmers have special difficulty receiving market signals because the agricultural production cycle is fairly rigid. Moreover, the scattered nature of China's farm household management at present has sharpened the contradictions in this aspect. Therefore, the government has the responsibility to help the farmers set up a suitable information system. By doing so, the individual households can make appropriate management decisions.

Storage system: Using this system to handle agricultural and sideline products, and control prices.

The contradictions between the relative decentralization of the supply of agricultural and sideline products and the centralization of demand for them often brings imbalances in the supply and demand situation, and this is clearly unfavorable for the stable increase of agricultural production. In order to safeguard the interests of the farmers it is necessary for the government to allocate a certain amount of money to improve the existing storage system, enlarge the handling ability and control prices.

Circulation system: Facilitating the circulation of agricultural and sideline products through wholesale and retail markets.

The rigidity of the production cycle, stemming from the traditional natural production rhythms of agriculture, causes farmers to fail to keep up with the market changes when they make their management decisions. All this has brought great difficulties for attaining equilibrium in the long-term supply of and demand for agricultural products. The solution is to set up exchanges of agricultural and sideline products. The short-term task is to set up and perfect wholesale markets for agricultural and sideline products, and the scale of futures will be gradually enlarged in regions that have superior conditions.

Processing system: Promoting the deep-processing of agricultural and sideline products, boosting added value and raising the all-round economic benefits of agriculture.

Agriculture is basically resource and labor intensive. But, while labor is plentiful in the rural areas, resources are not. Therefore, the government should help agricultural producers set up and perfect the processing system of agricultural and sideline products, promote the deep-processing of agricultural and side-

CHAPTER V CHANGING FUNCTIONS OF THE GOVERNMENT

line products, boost added value and raise the economic returns from agriculture.

Support system: To guarantee sustained high yields from agriculture, modern science and technology, and modern agricultural machinery will be used to provide a complete set of services for agriculture.

Limited land restricts the development of agricultural production in the present state of low agricultural technology. To meet the increasing demand for agricultural and sideline products, the government should set up a support system to provide new technologies, equipment, and other services for agricultural production.

2. The agricultural sphere indirectly affected by the government in the development of market agriculture.

Financial measures: regulation tax on industry and agriculture, and reduction of or exemption from agricultural tax.

The increase of labor productivity of agriculture always lags behind that of industry. For this reason, it is difficult to eliminate the price scissors existing in industrial and agricultural production. On the contrary, the price scissors is often widened. Therefore, agriculture is always at a relative disadvantage in the overall economic picture. But to ensure profits for agriculture, the government can increase the regulatory taxes for industry, while lowering those for agriculture to realize the balanced development of industry and agriculture.

Financial policy: The use of special-purpose loans from agricultural banks and upping non-governmental credit.

The return on agricultural investment often can not reach that on non-agriculture sectors. Therefore, the government must extend special support to agricultural investment, with the stress on long-term and basic investment for environmental and social benefit.

Welfare policy: Setting up organizations to provide agricultural and medical insurance in rural areas.

Agricultural production uses the whole of the natural environment as its production site. Therefore, agricultural production entails risks of natural calamities in addition to economic ones.

To enable farm households to withstand risks, the government should set up bodies to provide agricultural insurance, and extend special insurance coverage for crops that are seriously damaged by natural calamities.

Administrative legislation: Agricultural legislation for the protection of resources, support of prices, input of science and technology, etc.

Losses of agricultural resources, especially losses of cultivated land, have a damaging impact on efforts to ensure the long-term and stable growth of the national economy. Therefore, attention should be paid to protect agricultural resources.

(II) With the Objective of Quickening the Marketing of Agricultural Products, Macrocontrol Measures Should Be Perfected

The changing of the functions of the government should be speeded up, administrative control should be loosened and macro control should be conscientiously improved. Administrative measures applied by the government to control the supply of certain agricultural means of production should be abolished gradually. Supplies of agricultural means of production have been unstable, resulting in severe price fluctuations for agricultural products. Therefore, it is difficult to guarantee the supply of agricultural products, and also difficult to control price levels.

The government used to purchase a certain proportion of the major agricultural products such as grain and cotton, by compulsory administrative methods. This way of doing things is on the way out, as administrative interference worked to lower prices artificially. This in turn diluted the initiative of the farmers for planting grain crops and cotton, and an imbalance of supply and demand resulted. Another problem is that the holding down of prices artificially causes a price explosion when market forces are first allowed to operate.

The market economy in rural areas should be regulated by economic means.

Financial policy should focus on increasing the basic investment in agriculture, with reserve and risk funds set up. The

CHAPTER V CHANGING FUNCTIONS OF THE GOVERNMENT

purpose of the reserve fund is to regulate the circulation of the major agricultural products in order to stabilize the market; the risk fund is for emergency use, in case of war or natural disasters. Financial policy should also be coordinated with price policy, industrial policy and policy concerning foreign trade so as to stabilize the prices of agricultural products and promote export. In the meantime, tax policy should be oriented at strengthening the protection of agricultural production and rural incomes, and lightening the financial burden on farmers. In recent years farmers have been paying over 20 percent of their incomes in tax and miscellaneous fees. The various fees should be abolished. The agricultural tax rate should be at a level which can spur agricultural production as well as protect farmers' incomes in the conditions of the market economy. The tax rate should not be too high nor increase too quickly. When possible, agricultural tax can be reduced appropriately or exempted.

A rural monetary regulation system should be set up and perfected to guarantee financial credits for agriculture. Such a system should have a clear division of labor and close coordination among policy banks, commercial banks and cooperative financial organizations. When agricultural banks and rural cooperative banks operate completely in accordance with commercial management standards credit investment will favor the regions and industries with high rates of profit. For this reason, too much investment may flow into non-agricultural economic sectors. Therefore, the state should provide subsidies to the rural commercial banks, so those banks can make low-interest loans available to agricultural production. The price policy should be applied rationally, and the prices of agricultural products should be stabilized through stabilizing production. The objectively fair prices or the lowest protective prices should be determined in order to guide the market prices of agricultural products, stimulate the production of major agricultural products, and raise the farmers' income level.

China's comparative superiority in agriculture should be given full play, and the relations between supply and demand on agricultural product markets at home should be regulated by the trade policies of import and export of agricultural products. China's agricultural product markets should be linked to the international market. The state should adopt all kinds of policies and measures to give energetic support to the export of agricultural products, and encourage agricultural enterprises and rural economic organizations to directly export agricultural products. The distribution of export quotas should be implemented by public bidding. When necessary, export subsidies should be extended to agricultural products.

In a market economy agriculture is a weak sector. It has high social benefit but low benefit for the people engaged in it. Therefore, only if agriculture receives a certain amount of protection can it develop more rapidly. Since China's agricultural base is particularly weak, it especially needs state assistance.

The main problem in the development of the rural economy at present is that of agricultural protection. But from a long-term point of view over-protection of agriculture should be avoided as it will bring about a series of unfavorable side-effects. In the first place, China's agricultural population accounts for about 80 percent of the total population, so a protection policy means the minority protecting the majority, and the state does not have the financial capacity to solve this problem. Second, over-protection will stimulate production at high cost. It is not conducive either to optimizing the allocation of agricultural resources or to tightening management. Third, over-protection will cause a surplus of agricultural products. If the government takes the responsibility of absorbing this surplus it will find it a difficult financial burden. On the other hand, if it does not undertake the responsibility peasants will find it difficult to sell their grain, and sustain heavy losses. Fourth, over-protection hinders the linking of the domestic agricultural product markets with the international market.

No matter how agriculture is supported and protected by the government, in the end, the deciding factor is the strength of its competitiveness. So we have to speed up rural reform to meet the demands of the marketization of agricultural products, the growth of rural key-element markets and the development of

CHAPTER V CHANGING FUNCTIONS OF THE GOVERNMENT

township enterprises. When the competitive ability of agriculture has been strengthened the farmers can freely participate in market competition and their incomes will rise. Only in this way can their enthusiasm for production be further stimulated.

(III) Educating and Training Farmers Is an Important Governmental Function

The overall quality of China's agricultural workers is low. This has seriously restricted the transfer of achievements in science and technology to agriculture to increase productivity.

According to an estimate made by agricultural experts at the United Nations and in the United States, within 10 to 20 years only one sixth of the increase in agricultural products will come from the expansion of the area under cultivation, and the rest will come from biotechnical innovations. Since 1957 the total area under cultivation in China has been reduced year by year. Now it is impossible to expand the area under cultivation because new land resources are quickly becoming exhausted. For raising the total output of grain, the only way for China in the future is to raise the per unit area yield of grain. To achieve this aim, China needs to rely on the popularization and application of science and technology.

In the development of China's agriculture, the contribution rate of science and technology is very low, and is becoming lower, because at present the overall quality of China's agricultural workers is low. At present, there are about 340 million workers engaged in agriculture. Their educational levels are as follows: illiterates and semi-illiterates account for 24.99 percent; primary school graduates account for 38.4 percent; and junior middle school graduates account for 29.39 percent. Since 1949 more than 1.5 million agricultural technical personnel have been trained by secondary technical schools and colleges. But now less than 150,000 of these people are working in agriculture. Whereas over 90 percent of agricultural laborers in the United States, Germany and France have received vocational and technical training. In Japan 80 percent of young farmers have received senior middle school education, and in Britain over 60 percent of the agricultural laborers have received secondary agricultural school education. Agricultural training should be regarded as an important function of the government. One of the important tasks for the government is to organize and carry out all kinds of on-the-job education and training. The governments in Western countries work in coordination with non-governmental organizations in this respect. For us, their experiences are worth using for reference.

With the deepening of the reform in China's rural areas the consciousness of the importance of opening up among China's farmers has been strengthened, and they have a bigger desire for knowledge than ever before. At present, generally speaking, the cultural quality of China's rural people is fairly low, and a large number of such people need special technical training.

Increasing investment for education in rural areas is an important responsibility of the government. To this day, the educational conditions in China's rural areas are much worse than in urban areas. The reason is that the educational expenses in urban areas are borne by the government, but in rural areas they are borne by the local people themselves. Therefore, first of all, the government should increase its educational investment in rural areas.

Multi-channels are needed for carrying out agricultural training because of the scale and complications of the task. The centers for spreading agricultural science and technology at present should be changed into centers for agricultural training.

(IV) Building Legal Systems to Stabilize the Expectations of the Rural People

Stabilizing the psychological expectations of the masses of farmers is of vital importance for overall stabilization during the transition period of the economy. Great attention should be paid to this.

There have been great changes in the psychological expectations of the farmers during the transition from the traditional planned economy to a market economy. The relative instability

CHAPTER V CHANGING FUNCTIONS OF THE GOVERNMENT

brought about by market changes and policy readjustments have resulted in confusion about their lives and work among the farmers. This in turn directly influences the fluctuations of the market and the stability in rural areas.

Confidence among the farmers requires guarantees from systems and legislation. In recent years the pace of reform in China's rural areas has become fairly rapid, but the building of systems and the legal framework have lagged behind. The management in rural areas mostly relies on the traditional methods of control. The result is that the problems of the financial burden on farmers and infringements on their rights and interests continue unsolved. In addition, the farmers are always worried about possible changes in policies, because there is no basic legal system in place. So it is difficult for the farmers to make long-term input to agriculture. The most important measures for stabilizing the rural areas and the lives and work of the farmers are the strengthening of the legal system.

The basic laws for agriculture should be improved and perfected to reflect not only the basic policies and strategy of China's agricultural development, but also the reform achievements and the strides made in building the market economy in the rural areas.

Management regulations for land contracting in the rural areas need to be formulated. The existing contract responsibility system based on the household and with remuneration linked to output in the rural areas is determined by policy, but still lacks relevant laws. The contract responsibility system, as the basic measure and most important achievement of rural reform, urgently needs to be fixed by legal forms to give the farmers the right to use land for long periods of time, with their various rights and interests clearly stipulated and protected. The circulation of contracted land should also be stipulated and the land circulation market should be standardized. The relations between the collectives and farm households, and between the state and farm households should be made clear and definite.

The laws and regulations dealing with agricultural investment, macrocontrol, protection of resources, investment, popularization of science and technology, the market system, and intermediary organizations in rural areas also need to be formulated. The aim is to ensure that the reform in the rural areas and agricultural development can have laws and rules to follow. The building of the legal system in the rural areas is extremely complicated in market economy conditions, and it will take a long time. It is advisable to begin with experiments in village communities and, after these experiences have been analyzed, the results can be spread throughout the country.

The affairs of village communities should be managed according to laws, and a climate of public opinion built up which fully supports this way of doing things. Legal contracts should be drawn up to regulate the most important areas of rural life and work, such as family planning and management of enterprises. The process will be under the supervision of the local competent departments such as agricultural affairs commissions, family planning commissions and managerial stations. Village affairs commissions and farm households will sign contracts with each other, then the contracts will be notarized at notary offices. The farm households, village affairs commissions and local competent departments will each keep copies of the contracts.

With the quickening of rural modernization, especially the development of the rural market economy, new changes in the rural economy, social relations and contradictions have taken place. The rural economy has become more diversified and complicated than ever before. But although the methods and measures of management need to be renewed gradually, at present traditional managerial methods are still prevalent in China's rural areas. These methods result in the perpetuation of various types of irregularities such as banquets paid for with public funds, offering and demanding bribes. Though some laws and regulations, such as the Land Law, Mineral Resources Law and Tax Law have been promulgated for many years, yet illegal acts such as using farm land for non-agricultural purposes, reckless mining, evading taxes, are still fairly common in some places. In the present situation, if the conventional managerial methods continue to be used the contradictions and problems we face can not be

CHAPTER V CHANGING FUNCTIONS OF THE GOVERNMENT

solved either in whole or in part. In order to maintain the rapid pace of growth of the rural economy and promote the overall development of the society it is a matter of great urgency to study new managerial methods. As the state exercises the function of macro control over the market economy it must adhere to legal principles when applying economic and administrative measures. All economic management and all administrative orders must be institutionalized and put into a legal framework. Legal means only must be used to unify administrative and economic measures. Only when legal measures are strengthened can macro control be freed of reckless and blind decision-making. This means that Party committees and governments at different levels should manage the rural economy and society strictly in accordance with the law.

With the deepening of reform and the growing complexity of social relations in rural areas, many new problems have appeared. One of the difficult areas is family planning. All kinds of administrative measures and economic penalties, have been adopted, but unplanned births still take place, especially in remote areas. Again, despite repeated orders and instructions from the government, the problem of the financial burden on farmers has still not been solved; in many places the problem has even become more serious. The main reason for this situation is that the law enforcement departments handle these contradictions and problems by means of administrative intervention. Besides, many administrative cadres lack sufficient legal knowledge and personal factors are often allowed to intrude on the administration of law enforcement. In the past administrative measures were used to solve all kinds of social problems and all kinds of economic problems. But such problems are not solved very well by administrative measures. On the contrary, some contradictions have been intensified because of such an approach. Establishing a sound legal system is the only recourse for China in its advance toward becoming a thoroughly modern society.

China's ancient society was set up on the basis of private ownership, but no legal guarantees concerning property were ever set up.

THE REFORM AND DEVELOPMENT OF CHINA'S RURAL ECONOMY

In ancient China contracts were formed within communities in the countryside to standardize people's behavior. Things were different outside communities. There was no civil law. Therefore, there was a great deal of arbitrariness as concerns property controversies, negotiations, notarization and judgment. There was no way to restrict violations of property rights, especially by officials. Most of the feudal dynasties concentrated power at the center. This was beneficial for unifying and administering China, but it institutionalized intervention by the authorities in every sphere of life. After the founding of New China in 1949 there were many things waiting to be done. Socialist reform began immediately, and at that time there was no time for the government to formulate civil laws. In China's rural areas, within only a few years, people's communes with collective ownership were set up all over the country. At the beginning of the era of people's communes a publicly-owned land system was implemented. Most of the peasants did not join on a voluntary basis. But they did not make a stand against the communes, nor did they demand rules and regulations that could protect their interests be worked out. At that time they were all in favor of collectivization. But later they tried to sabotage the communes when they found that they could not leave them of their own free will. Unlawful behavior, such as being slack at work, stealing public property and taking more than one's share, was common. They tried by every means to gain extra advantage by unfair means. If after land reform property rights had been defined by legislation and the farmers had known that they had the right to protect their own property the situation would have been much better. If their property rights had been violated they would have learned how to handle things according to law. They would have held negotiations between the parties concerned, asked notary organs for help, or even gone to court. The Party and the government could have found out the bonding point of the farmers' common and individual interests. After that policies would have been formulated and the problems of subjectivism, commandism and issuing confusing orders avoided. In this situation the farmers would have been able to make stable production arrangements, work hard,

CHAPTER V CHANGING FUNCTIONS OF THE GOVERNMENT

improve farm management and invest more in their land. So it is clear that defining rights is favorable to forming markets of key elements of production and optimizing the allocation of resources. The definition of rights should always accompany the making of policies. Since the implementation of the household contract system it has become imperative to separate the rights of ownership and management. The ownership of the land should belong to the collective, while the rights of operation, management and usufruct should belong to the farm households. Contracted rights should not be changed for 30 years. Use rights should be able to be transferred for compensation, used as mortgage pledges or converted into stock.

(V) The Development of the Rural Market Economy Needs Stronger Control Based on the Law of the Market

As the market economy in China is still in the initial stage, some policies have not yet been perfected. Thus confusion in market order exists in some regions and in some trades. Bogus products and products of inferior quality are found everywhere, much to the consumers' annoyance. Some departments even use their functions and powers to seek their own interests at the expense of the general public. Only legal regulation of the economy according to market norms can remove such irregularities.

II. The Development of Rural Industrialization

(I) Industrialization of the Rural Economy Is the Strategic Orientation for the Further Development of Agriculture

Promoting the industrialization of the rural economy is the focus of the development of agriculture at present. It is also necessary for making agriculture gain the initiative in market competition, for promoting the combination of industry and agriculture and town and country, and for making historical progress.

The object is the comprehensive exploitation of agricultural resources and the optimization of labor utilization on the premise that the urban and rural sectors promote complementarity. Agricultural industrialization is the basic trend for the development of modern agriculture. Maintaining the stable development of agriculture and building up the capacity for sustained agricultural development are common pursuits in many countries at present. First, science and technology are being applied increasingly in agricultural production. Modern agricultural science and technology are expanding swiftly to both the macro and micro spheres in an all-round way. The exclusive dependence on the investment of traditional resources will be gradually replaced by the input of science and technology, which will increasingly become the initiative factor in agricultural development. On this basis the old closed systems will become open ones and the combination of town and country will be promoted, as will large-scale circulation and markets. There will be a clear-cut process of three stages in agriculture: pre-production, production and post-production. The combination of trade, industry and agriculture, and agriculture, science and education will enable new industries to be gradually created. On top of this will come commercialization, internationalization and the production of high-grade items.

The development of agriculture must always take into account market needs. Natural resources should be exploited and used comprehensively, yet in a sustainable way, and the variety of marketable agricultural and sideline products should be expanded. Key industries should be fostered, as should a processing industry with high added value.

Agricultural industrialization is a realistic channel for solving the deep contradictions in China's agriculture. In the past 18 years of reform and opening up the comprehensive productive ability and integral quality of agriculture have been greatly raised. But there are still difficulties and problems in the course of development. The prominent contradictions are as follows: First, the growing demand for agricultural products and the weak foundation of agriculture. Judging by the population increase trend at present and in the future, and the trends in consumer

CHAPTER V CHANGING FUNCTIONS OF THE GOVERNMENT

demand and industrial development, the demand for agricultural products will continue to show a powerful upward momentum. If agriculture wants to play a really fundamental and supporting role in the development of the national economy it must keep sustained and stable development, and its comprehensive production ability needs to increase substantially. But the actual situation is that in recent years investment in agriculture has been unsatisfactory, and has even decreased, and the speed of the transformation and renewal of the basic agricultural installations is slow. Second, the development of agriculture has produced comparatively low benefits. Agriculture, in fact, is the least profitable of all China's economic sectors and it is difficult for it to share in the general prosperity fairly and reasonably. This will result in the diversion of elements of production—labor, funds, technology, and land. Third, there are problems guaranteeing supplies and increasing incomes. With the imbalance in comparative benefits and the discrepancies in the market environment, the farmers' enthusiasm for engaging in non-agricultural pursuits and diversifying the economy in order to increase their incomes has surpassed that for producing grain and cotton. It is fairly difficult to guarantee the supply of the main agricultural products—grain and cotton. Fourth, raising labor productivity and increasing employment opportunities. If agricultural specialization, commercialization and modernization are to be promoted labor productivity must be raised. But the present channels of employment for the rural labor force are narrow, and the rise of labor productivity threatens to reduce the job opportunities for the large rural labor force even further.

These contradictions are, in the final analysis, problems of the realization of agricultural value and accumulation ability, problems of the combination and disposition of agricultural resources and elements of production, and the problems of interest relations between city and countryside, and industry and agriculture. The fundamental way to solve these problems is to promote agricultural industrialization, the coordination of social and agricultural benefit, and the combination of production and operation activities. Market circulation should be linked to individual production and operating activities and integration of operations. Traditional agriculture will move in the direction of becoming large-scale agriculture; the traditional separation of cities and countryside will change into integration of cities and countryside; and the vigor of agriculture will be increased along with the raising of the degree of organization of the farmers. This will enable agriculture to participate in market competition and distribution of resources on an equal footing, and share the fruits of the development of the national economy as a whole.

Agricultural industrialization is the objective requirement of rural reform and development. In the early 1980s the implementation of the contract responsibility system based on the household and with remuneration linked to output brought about an improvement in the rural relations of production, and the liberation of the productive forces. In the mid-1980s the readjustment of the economic structure brought about a re-organization of the factors of production and an overall enlivening of the economy. The rural market economy and the building of market agriculture being carried on at present mark a new stage in the rural reform. The result will be profound changes and an overall development of agriculture and the rural areas. But it is necessary to keep in mind that the reform process is related to the readjustment of interests and the redisposal of all kinds of economic resources. One problem that must be solved is how to guide farmers toward production suitable the needs of market changes in order to enable scattered production to integrate with a large-scale market? Another is how to raise the competitiveness of agricultural products, the economic benefits of agriculture and managerial efficiency of the market for agricultural products? In the readjustment of the rural industrial structure, how are we to fully develop and make use of natural resources, and make sure that secondary and tertiary industry and agriculture develop in a balanced way? The industrialization of agriculture and the rural economy will help promote the compartmentalization and specialization of agricultural production, and raise the degree of agricultural commercialization. It will also help raise the degree of organization of agricultural production and strengthen the

CHAPTER V CHANGING FUNCTIONS OF THE GOVERNMENT

capacity of farm households to sustain market risks. In addition, it will promote the processing and circulation of agricultural products, raise the economic benefits of agriculture and raise its accumulation and development capacity. Finally it will help promote cooperation between workers and peasants and between cities and the countryside, and quicken the building of agricultural modernization and rural industrialization.

The development of the rural economy along the lines of industrialization marks not only a new leap forward for the rural productive forces but also a profound change in the relations of rural production. Therefore, the period of the transition of agriculture and the rural economy to a socialist market economy entails certain contradictions.

First, the contradiction between farm households and the market. The development of the market economy needs well-knit organizations and well-conceived plans. But at present China's farmers are engaged in decentralized and small-scale production. Thus the big problem at present is how to guide farmers to embrace the market economy, and how to solve the contradiction between the scattered production of farm households and the large-scale social market. The experience of some places in Shandong Province has proved that pursuing the industrialization of agriculture and the rural economy is the effective way to solve the problem. The system of contracted responsibility on the household basis and with remuneration linked to output will not be changed. But on the basis of industrialization, the degree of organization of the farmers will be raised, and the scale, specialization, socialization and integration of agriculture and the rural economy will be realized. Experiments in certain places have proved that the market economy is not without organization and without plans. It needs, in fact, strict organization and well-conceived plans. Agricultural production must accord with the demands of markets both at home and abroad. The variety, quality and specification must accord with the demands of order forms; chickens are cut into different parts—over 100 varieties; vegetables are processed into different specifications—dozens of varieties. This shows that only organizations of industrialization (not scattered households) can conform to and control the market.

Second, the contradiction between small-scale management of agriculture and realization of agricultural modernization must be solved. At present, the managerial scale of agriculture is fairly small, and this is the main factor restricting the improvement of the quality of agricultural science and technology, and equipment. The industrialization provides the possibility of solving this contradiction. So long as industrialization brings in advanced technology market competitiveness will be raised, leading to higher foreign exchange earnings.

Third, the contradiction between decentralized management and scale management, and that between scattered household management and intensive farming must be solved. In the conditions of the market economy the management of farm households can not be restricted to self-sufficiency; the situation requires that they should bring their operations within the scope of large-scale production through scale management and intensive farming. Scale management not only means scale management of land, but also the constant enlargement of management scale through combination to better suit the needs of socialized large-scale production.

Fourth, the contradiction of the separation of town and country. Industrialization puts a premium on skilled people, technology and funds, and helps to optimize rural resources and labor power. The common interests formed by urban enterprises, and rural economic bases and farm households promote the urbanization process in rural areas, and also strengthen enterprises' operations, service capacity and radiation capacity. The industrialization of agriculture and the rural economy, and the development of leading enterprises also can promote the development of the construction of small cities and towns, and the process of the integration of town and country.

Fifth, the contradiction between the high-level social impact of agriculture and its own low-level benefits. The comparative benefits of agriculture are low, so farmers' enthusiasm for production is not high. In the conditions of a market economy this is the outstanding restrictive factor. The realistic choice for raising the comparative benefits of agriculture is the implementation of industrialization, devoting major efforts to developing some leading enterprises, such as enterprises dealing with agricultural processing and storage.

(II) Grain Production Should Be Modernized

Modernizing agriculture means that agriculture, especially grain production, should be developed into a modernized economic sector, integrating trade, industry, agriculture and technology, and combining the production, supply and marketing of products. China's present agricultural situation is that of a small-scale peasant economy marked by self-supply, self-production and self-support. The entrenched planned economy ensured the leading role of administration; the supply of agricultural capital, and grain purchase, processing and sales were separated from agricultural production and divided into different government departments in charge of their management (the supply and marketing cooperatives have actually become economic sectors of the government). This runs counter to the rules for the development of modernized large-scale agriculture, which needs the application of modern science and technology, and the combination of production, supply and marketing of products. It is sometimes said that the United States has advanced agriculture because less manpower supports more people. Actually, this is not entirely true. There are 2.5 million people engaged in agricultural production there, but the pre- and post-production agricultural employees total 25 million; farm production accounts for only one tenth of the total employment in agriculture in the US. People employed in pre-production services (producing and supplying chemical fertilizer, farm chemicals and farm machinery) number five million, accounting for 20 percent of the total; post-production personnel (in purchasing, processing, stockpiling, transportation and sales) number 17.5 million, accounting for 70 percent of the total. This massive labor and management contingent is linked together by the bonds of the market economy. But in China, pre- and post-production services are separated from farm production. People engaged in farm production only provide grain, raw cotton and rapeseed; they do not engage in value-added preliminary processing. In addition, commodity grain is purchased at low prices.

In 1994 the State Council stipulated that the purchasing price of grain by the government should be raised, in order to spur the farmers' enthusiasm for planting grain crops. But price rises for agricultural materials far exceeded the grain price rise, so grain on the market was priced far higher than the government stipulated. Therefore, the industrialization of agriculture is imperative, along with the integration of supply, production and marketing of products. In fact, some places have set up some key industries (production and processing of meat, vegetables, aquatic products, etc.) which are closely connected with agriculture and provide preliminary experience for the industrialization of agriculture.

The organizational form of industrialized agriculture should be group stock-holding companies or stock-holding agriculture (or companies producing and processing grain, oil, vegetables, meat, etc.), based mainly on publicly-owned assets. Then the combination of science and technology with production can be more easily accomplished and investment in science and technology increased. The content of science and technology in foodstuffs production will rise to 50 percent at the end of this century from 30 percent at present, and will even reach 70-80 percent of that of the developed countries at the beginning of the next century.

Group companies for the production and processing of meat will be set up and major efforts will be devoted to developing the production and marketing of animal husbandry.

The key to the industrialization of agriculture is ensuring that each link reaps a reasonable profit. If administrative measures are mainly relied on, with supply and marketing at limited prices, there will be a critical shortage of agricultural materials (especially chemical fertilizer) and the enthusiasm for production of the households planting grain crops will be dampened. The result will be a shortage of agricultural products. Therefore,

CHAPTER V CHANGING FUNCTIONS OF THE GOVERNMENT

certain countermeasures should be adopted: 1) Tax exemptions and reductions should be granted by departments supplying agricultural materials, or subsidies may be given to in accordance with market prices (keeping average profit). 2) Grain price controls should be lifted and grain coupons marked at state-set prices given to impoverished urban citizens. Of course, China's grain prices can not exceed international grain prices, otherwise large quantities of grain will pour into China, posing a challenge to China's agriculture and raising international grain prices at the same time. 3) A completely modern industrialized agriculture should be aimed at, with the combination of supply, production and marketing of products. This will simplify the intermediate links and place a large number of surplus rural workers in new employment. Thereby efficiency will be greatly raised and operation expenses reduced.

(III) Making Full Use of International and Domestic Markets, and Optimizing the Structure of Rural Industry

The present market price of domestic wheat is close to the price of imported wheat including insurance and freight costs. The same tendency in other grain varieties will appear sooner or later. If China's grain price passes this point the domestic grain production structure (mainly self-supporting and self-sufficient) as well as the consumption structure will come to a standstill. China not only does not have the ability to subsidize grain production but its steady economic growth depends on the rapid modernization of agriculture. The main basis of this argument is as follows: As population increases and the area of arable land shrinks the farmers who grow grain and other staple crops are left at a disadvantage. For example: Planting one *mu* wheat takes 15 working days. If the net income per working day is 10 yuan, that means a total income of 150 yuan for planting one *mu*. If each unit of labor power occupies three *mu*, then the income will be 450 yuan, and if two crops are reaped a year the annual income per farmer will be only 900 yuan. A three-member family depending on 900 yuan a year is regarded as a poverty-stricken household. However, less land is needed for animal husbandry, aquaculture or the production of cash crops. The same is true for industry and trade. Even if the pay is only about 10 yuan a day each person can work for 150, 200 or even 300 days a year. This means that the average annual income per unit of labor force can reach 1,500, 2,000 or 3,000 yuan. The comparative benefit of grain production and other main agricultural products is fairly low. Therefore, the production of items connected with grain and other agricultural products can not make full use of China's cheap and abundant labor force. On the other hand, countries with less people and more land (expensive labor and relatively cheap land) find that it is worthwhile to grow grain both because of economies of scale and comparative benefits. In this situation it is better for China to devote its land and labor to the production of items with better economic results. At the same time, grain can be imported both from places which have many people and little land and advanced countries with comparatively few people and sufficient land. With transportation, foreign currency exchange, markets for products and timely information arranged appropriately, the market mechanism can be employed to solve this problem.

Over the past decade or so the reform of the agricultural structure has been accompanied by an increase in population, decrease in cultivated land and grain crop area, and no particular increase in per unit area yield of grain crops. Yet there has been a remarkable improvement in the diet of the ordinary Chinese people. Why is this? The reason is that in recent years animal husbandry, aquaculture, fisheries, orchard planting and other agricultural side-occupations have developed rapidly. These new development spheres of agriculture have grown swiftly because the market mechanism propels them smoothly, they are profit-oriented, and every link of production, supply and marketing of products can absorb the investment of resources. Thus a favorable situation quickly takes shape. A more important thing is that, compared with grain production, these aspects of agriculture can furnish extra employment. It is a process of spontaneous change and shows that the agricultural structure is changing under market regulation, leading to solutions to two problems—sluggish food supply growth and increased rural unemployment. Following this path, double the fruits can be attained with half the effort.

The readjustment of the industrial structure involves readjustment of the proportions of basic and other sectors of industry, optimized allocation of resources, and synchronized and coordinated development of all aspects. By satisfying market demand, industry will reap more benefits. But the readjustment of industry must accord with the requirements of economic laws and be in tune with economic development. We cannot ignore objective reality; blind readjustment will be penalized by economic laws. The readjustment of the structure of agriculture in the direction of industrialization should adhere to the general laws mentioned above. But agriculture's strategic position and its low comparative benefits should be taken into account in the meanwhile.

III. Coordinated Development of Urban and Rural Areas

(I) From Now On, the Rural Market Should Spur the Urban Market, While Coordinated Development of Urban and Rural Areas Should Be Promoted

The task facing us is to deepen the rural economic reform while changing the track of the whole economic system. It is essential for the rural economy to adopt a market orientation, which will in turn promote the building of the market economy in urban areas. Agriculture is the base for the sustained development of the whole national economy. Without the further development of the rural economy it will be impossible to create good conditions for changing the track of the whole national economy. The development of the rural economy can only depend on the thorough reform of the rural economic system in the direction of the market. This will bring about a readjustment of the rural industrial structure, the transfer of surplus rural labor, the enlargement of rural markets and the rise of rural purchasing power. In turn, it will stimulate the urban economy by creating a competitive situation and development opportunities, promoting urban reform.

(II) The Development Strategy for Industry and Agriculture: from Agriculture Nurturing Industry to Industrial and Agricultural Exchanges at Equal Values, and Gradually to Industry Nurturing Agriculture

The basic problem we face in the process of industrialization is how to speed up the development of industry on the premise of not damaging agriculture but promoting it. This is also the starting point in formulating the economic development strategy. In the first few decades of New China we adopted the development strategy of agriculture nurturing industry. The prices of foodstuffs and of most light industrial materials (as agricultural products) were reduced as a matter of policy. Thus, a high rate of accumulation was realized. But eventually, if this strategy had continued to be followed, industry would have been deprived of rural consumer markets and raw agricultural materials and products, thus slowing down industrial development. Therefore, the development strategy for industry and agriculture had to be readjusted. At the present stage the products of industry and agriculture should be exchanged at equal value; industry and agriculture should develop evenly; the price scissors between industry and agriculture should be narrowed; and gradually the situation should be changed into one in which industry nurtures agriculture.

In this process the estrangement of city and countryside will be abolished, along with the system of household registration which used to segregate the cities from the countryside. Farmers will be allowed to settle in urban areas, obtaining employment, setting up enterprises and buying or building houses. Experiments are being made first of all in small cities and towns in order to control the expansion of population in big and medium-sized cities.

(III) In Macro Control of Agriculture by the Government Special Emphasis Will Be Laid on Readjusting the Eco-

CHAPTER V CHANGING FUNCTIONS OF THE GOVERNMENT

nomic Relations Between Industry, Agriculture, the Cities, the Countryside and the State

In recent years, facing a series of problems such as the sluggish development of agriculture, slow growth of farmers' incomes and the continuous worsening of the ecological environment in the countryside, the government has taken a series of measures. But the results have not been satisfactory because the macroeconomic environment of agricultural production has not fundamentally improved and all kinds of economic relations are in a state of imbalance. Agriculture should be given priority in economic work and its sustained development ensured.

1. Relations between industry and agriculture.

Industry and agriculture are the two pillars of the national economy. Whether or not the relations between the two are coordinated exerts a tremendous influence on the development of industrial and agricultural production, and the development of the whole national economy. China's industrialization started under special historical conditions—a very weak national economic base and almost total isolation from the outside world. So there was no other way to develop industry apart from using the price scissors of industrial and agricultural products. The development of industry depended on sacrificing the development of agriculture. The price scissors left over by history has remained too long; it has increased by too big a margin, and the relations between industry and agriculture have been seriously distorted. As the situation changed and industry started to gain the capacity for self-accumulation, the state did not carry out the readjustment of industrial policies in time. On the one hand, under the conditions of excessive price scissors and a big gap between the comparative advantages of industry and agriculture, the development of industry has been fast for a long time. Not only has large-city industry developed swiftly, but town and township industry has also begun to speed up its development. But the internal motive power of agricultural development is insufficient, the wastage of agricultural resources is serious and its development speed can not suit the needs of the development of industry.

On the other hand, the slow development of agriculture not only restricts the further development of the industrial economy, it also narrows the market for industrial products in rural areas. The rapid increase of the productive capacity of industry has formed a sharp contrast to the situation mentioned above. In the internal structure of industry the sector of farm-oriented means of production is restricted by the narrow agricultural market. So its scale is difficult to enlarge and its economic benefits are difficult to raise. The prices of agricultural products have been raised by a big margin several times, but the speed can not catch up with that of the rise in prices of farm-oriented means of production. Poor-quality and high-price industrial products have pushed up the production costs of agricultural products, enlarging the gap in comparative advantage between agriculture and non-agriculture, and slowing the increase in farmers' incomes. All this has dampened the enthusiasm of farmers. From this we can see that if we want to coordinate properly the relations between industry and agriculture, first of all the state must fundamentally change the tendency of laying stress on industry at the expense of agriculture, and readjust the relations of economic advantage between the two pillars of the economy.

2. Relations between city and countryside.

In the process of industrialization China has formed a dualist social structure by means of a series of concrete social systems isolating the cities from the countryside. The main barrier is the household registration system. Chinese society has been divided into the agricultural population and urban population. The former find themselves in disadvantageous positions as regards employment, education, and medical treatment. It is difficult for agricultural labor power to move to cities and towns. Since the 1980s, with the emergence of rural enterprises and small cities and towns, there has been a tide of rural labor moving to the cities, and this poses a challenge to the traditional isolation of town and country. But the problem remains.

3. Relations between the state and the rural population.

The farmers are the most positive, active and creative factor among the various agricultural productive forces. In China's

CHAPTER V CHANGING FUNCTIONS OF THE GOVERNMENT

present rural economic system farmers are not only the producers of agricultural products, but also the operators of agricultural enterprises. The actions of the farmers decide the situation of agricultural production and the agricultural development. In a nutshell, the actions of farmers decide whether agriculture burgeons or declines. During the period of socialist construction the core of farmers' problems was that of economic advantage, which hinged on the economic relations between the state and the farmers. At present, the contradiction between the state and the farmers is mainly manifested in the situation in which the state gets more from the farmers than it gives them. But now that the farmers are breaking away from planned forms of the economy and are embracing the market economy, the state finds itself in an ambiguous position vis-a-vis the farmers. On the one hand the state leads the farmers in organizing production according to the demands of the market in order to increase their incomes; on the other, the state has to use some administrative measures to ensure the output of agricultural products which are important to the nation's economy and the people's livelihood but not very profitable. The result is that the farmers are insecure because they know that government policy changes could affect their livelihoods at any time. The solution is for the state to deal with the farmers according to market laws, ensuring that they earn reasonable incomes while contributing agricultural products to the state.

(IV) Reform and Development

During the process of developing the agricultural productive forces over a long period of time, old systems have gradually been displaced by new ones. In brief, there are two aspects to this:

One aspect is the microeconomic sphere. With the progress of modernization, the small-scale and decentralized management involved in the household contract system becomes progressively at odds with the demands of modernization. But the rural policies should be stable; the agricultural household contract system can not lightly be changed. The contradiction can be solved only with the progress of agricultural modernization. Through agricultural-industrial-commercial integration, decentralized agricultural management will be linked up according to the demands of the market so that agricultural products from scattered farm households can be processed. Therefore, each farm household is required to produce agricultural products according to the needs of the processing industry. By doing so, agricultural production will be able to fulfill the demands of the market and the decentralized family management of farms will be brought into the production system, in accordance with the demands of society. Thus, the small-scale production of each farm household will become a compositional link in agricultural-industrial-commercial integration. In this process the managerial scale of farm households also will be enlarged gradually. This process means that socialization of agricultural production will be realized on the basis of farm household management. In most of China's rural areas the reform prospects can be predicted, and at the same time agricultural collective management will also be implemented in some rural areas having a higher managerial level, more non-agricultural economic sectors and a higher level of mechanization of agriculture. Now, each province has some villages with good collective agricultural management. But the pace of this process is slow and gradual.

The other aspect is the macroeconomic sphere. The aim of reform is to replace the local isolated and crude market economy featuring undue administrative interference with one featuring unified macro control. This process of replacement requires the following series of steps. A legal system administration suited to market needs should be set up, as does an effective macrocontrol system, business forecasting and other information networks, as well as communications and transportation. In the process of replacement we must be careful to maintain equilibrium of supply of and demand for agricultural products in total quantity and in structure. At the same time, the cultural and educational level of the farmers must be steadily raised.

In the past the government directly interfered in the operations of agriculture. Now it should change its function to one of developing the market, perfecting laws and regulations, executing the law, implementing measures to protect agriculture and build-

CHAPTER V CHANGING FUNCTIONS OF THE GOVERNMENT

ing up basic market facilities.

The farmers, in turn, should make every effort to increase agricultural production and raise its efficiency, and at the same time raise their cultural and educational levels. By so doing, their work and lives can conform to the modern market economy system. The task of building the modern market economy system will be accomplished by the new generation of farmers who have education.

(V) Development Is the Major Task for China's Rural Areas

1. Rural areas not only need to be reformed, they also need to be developed.

Reform will be conducted during the development. But does this mean that reform will be put in second place? The question will be decided by the stages of reform and development.

In 1978 China entered a new period of reform and opening up. It will be a long historical period, and there should be several stages in it. For example, in the first stage, the household contract system was rapidly carried out. After that, rural reform entered a stage which needed the drive of urban reform, and rural reform also impelled the development of agricultural production. Therefore, the pace of rural reform was slow, and rural reform even waited for urban reform.

China's rural areas had already completed their first stage of reform when the First Plenary Session of the 12th Central Committee of the Chinese Communist Party made the decision to go ahead with urban economic reform in October 1984. When the industrial enterprises in cities intended to reform their managerial systems the rural areas had already finished their managerial system reform. Therefore, the rural reform was not conducted in step with the urban reform.

The rural reform in the early 1980s stimulated the enthusiasm of the farmers, and promoted the swift increase of agricultural production, bringing about far-reaching effects on the urban areas and Chinese society and economy as a whole.

First, agricultural production. The implementation of the household management contract system in rural areas has achieved good results. Contracting land has aroused the initiative of the farmers, but at the same time the scale benefits of agriculture have been sacrificed because the land has become divided up into many scattered units. Therefore, the first step in rural reform has concealed factors hampering further development. To solve this hidden peril, after the first step of rural reform, in order to support the economic reform and development of urban areas and the whole country, great efforts must be made to develop the agricultural productive forces and agricultural output.

Second, the labor force in rural areas. The rural reform has enabled the broad masses of farmers to become independent commodity producers, thereby creating a micro-basis for the development of the rural commodity economy. Besides, the rural reform has enabled millions of farmers to shake off the yoke of the system of the communes and become free laborers. On the one hand, this is a benefit because these people provide abundant cheap labor for the development of both urban and rural industry, and they have been supporting the economic advance of the coastal developed areas. On the other hand, the shift of the rural labor force to cities and industry drains the countryside of young and relatively educated workers. This means that agriculture will suffer and there could be a shortage of agricultural products unless more investment is poured into agriculture and its productivity raised.

2. Agricultural development has great significance for urban reform.

The speed of urban reform will dictate the speed of rural reform from now on. But agricultural development will support or even promote urban reform.

Though the first step in rural reform touched off the urban reform and reforms in industry, it only did so by introducing the spirit of reform. The household contract system as practiced in the rural areas is difficult to apply in the urban and industrial sectors.

In the early 1980s the basic experience of the success in rural reform could be summed up like this: The success of reform led 90 percent of farmers to appreciate its advantages, as they per-

CHAPTER V CHANGING FUNCTIONS OF THE GOVERNMENT

sonally benefit from owning and selling what they produce. But China is a society with a binary economy, the twin pillars of which are agriculture and industry. The urban areas are dominated by industrialization and the commodity economy. The means of production there can not be divided up and contracted by the workers. The practice of contract management in industry is still controversial. As enterprises go bankrupt or are taken over by others many workers become redundant, which affect the urban reform. The pace of urban reform will dictate the pace of the next step of reform in the rural areas.

But agriculture is not entirely in a passive position. Although the next step in rural reform—establishing a market economy and reforming the circulation system—must follow urban reform, the development of agriculture can support urban reform.

How can agriculture promote urban reform? It can do so because agriculture develops at a different rate from industry. The history of China's economic development over the past decade or so has shown that when the speed of industrial development and urban construction surpass a certain limit inflation is triggered, followed by readjustment and tightening of the economy.

Though sometimes farm products are difficult to sell when agricultural production increases, inflation can be controlled. At the same time, increased production can create a comfortable environment for urban reform. So we can say that the development of agriculture is able to support and promote urban reform.

In order to avoid losses by farmers, market information, protection, and macroeconomic control should be provided by the government.

(VI) The Key to Rural Development Is Raising the Cultural Standards of the Peasants

China's rural economy can advance swiftly and vigorously because of the correct policies of the Party and the government, and their proper guidance. In the rural areas the system of people's communes has been abrogated; the system of contracted responsibilities on the household basis and with remuneration linked to output has been implemented; the policy of state monopoly of the purchase and marketing of grain has been put in abeyance; the prices of oil and grain, and market circulation have been decontrolled; the development of rural enterprises is encouraged and supported; some people are allowed to become prosperous before others; help-the-poor policies have been implemented; communications have been improved; water-conservancy projects have been built; improved varieties of farm plants have been popularized; and adequate legislation for agriculture has been enacted. All these have promoted the swift development of the rural economy.

But sometimes, people neglect something important, i.e., the development of the economy is connected with the internal factors motivating the farmers themselves. Correct policy guidance and support of the economy and materials are external factors, and it is an attitudinal change in the farmers themselves that is the driving power of the rural reform. Over the past decade, the farmers' attitudes have changed in the following way.

First, the awakening of farmers' subjective consciousness is the first important step. The "big-pot" distribution system (messing together) during the days of collectivization of agriculture tended to erode the initiative of the farmers for a long time. The "big-pot" system encouraged the development of sluggish factors. After the introduction of the reform and opening up policies the system of people's communes was abrogated, and the system of contracted responsibility on the household basis, with remuneration linked to output, was implemented. The farmers now have the right to use the land independently. They hand in a certain amount of their products to the state and the collectives, and the rest belongs to themselves. Thus, their initiative has been awakened. From 1979 to 1984 the yearly average production increase of grain was over 15 billion kg and that of cotton over 1.3 million *dan* (1 *dan*=50kg). In the early 1980s the farmers were still rooted in the small-scale peasant economy mentality. But with the development of the national economy the self-sufficient attitude of farmers has gradually changed to a more open one oriented to the market economy.

CHAPTER V CHANGING FUNCTIONS OF THE GOVERNMENT

Second, the change in the idea of the desirability of "sticking to the land." Nowadays farmers have little hesitation about leaving the land, because job opportunities are opening up all over the country in non-agricultural sectors. Some 50-70 million rural laborers pour into cities each year. The great change in the ideology of the farmers, the remolding of their social roles of peasants, and the change to a modernized outlook are what modern society needs. Rural laborers have supported the construction of the cities and at the same time they have widened their outlook, and have acquired money and a large amount of information on science and technology and managerial methods, which they take back with them to the countryside.

The rise of rural enterprises has reflected the switch from regarding agriculture as of basic importance. Now in the countryside there is a trend toward agricultural-industrial-commercial integration and a coordinated process of production, supply and marketing of products. At present, China has 23 million rural enterprises. These enterprises have recruited more than 100 million surplus rural workers and now create 36 percent of China's total industrial output value. The most important thing is that, with the creation of rural enterprises, farmers have taken a self-remolding road for rural economic development, the realization of rural industrialization and rural modernization.

Third, population growth in rural areas has been controlled because of the weakening of patriarchal authority. To rural dwellers the family planning policy has been a difficult one to carry out. Since the early 1980s the government has taken family planning as a basic policy to be carried out nationwide. Governments and women's federations at all levels have done a lot of work in this regard, i.e., by persuading rural people that the old ideas that "the more children one has, the happier one's lot," and "a son is needed to continue one's family line" have been changed into "fewer children and take better care of them." This reflects a fundamental change in patriarchal ideas, ethical attachment to one's family and concept of value among rural people. Especially, peasants in the regions where the economy is comparatively well developed have conscientiously accepted these new ideas. Gradually, they have become happy to accept the one-child family policy. Furthermore, the living standard of these families has been raised because their burdens have been lessened. This has weakened patriarchal ideas and changed the traditional values of the farmers a great deal. For these reasons, the birth rate in rural areas has declined by 15 per thousand (from 33.34 percent to 18.90 percent) over the past decade—the lowest birth rate among the developing countries.

Fourth, the raising of the farmers' cultural standards has been an important support for the take-off of the rural economy. According to statistics, China now has 66 agricultural colleges and universities, which have 114,845 undergraduates receiving professional training, and 3,477 postgraduates. In addition, there are 370 special agricultural technical secondary schools, which have 210,000 students. China has 16 branches of the Central Institute for Agricultural Administrators, 36 agricultural broadcasting schools and 2,298 agricultural schools at prefectural and city levels. These schools have 520,000 students. There are more than 2,000 county-level agricultural technology training centers and more than 40,000 township-level culture and technology schools for farmers. These educational organs have trained a large number of qualified people for the rural areas. Besides, there are more than 220,000 stations for popularizing agricultural technology, which have 1,177,000 technicians. These stations have trained 1,030,000 peasant technical personnel. These technical personnel have made important contributions to the popularization of agricultural science and technology, to the development of new products and to the setting up and management of rural enterprises.

The human factors mentioned above are important reasons for the swift development of the rural economy. Human factors are also responsible for the barriers which still exist in the way of economic progress in the rural areas.

The biggest obstacle to the development of the rural economy is the low cultural level in the rural areas, where there are some 200 million illiterate and semi-illiterate persons. Less than 20 percent of rural people have received more than secondary school

CHAPTER V CHANGING FUNCTIONS OF THE GOVERNMENT

education, and very few have received higher education. Therefore, promoting advanced science and technology and the comprehensive opening up of agricultural resources are difficult to coordinate with the development of the market economy. The entrenched methods of producing traditional items, preliminary processing and selling on domestic markets are the materialized reflection of this low level of culture, science and technology. The low cultural level of the farmers has also resulted in low organizational ability. Before the setting up of safety measures for agriculture, the interests of the farmers may be harmed when conflicts of interest take place among different strata. When they meet market risks they instinctively turn back to the natural economy; on the threshold of the market, they take a passive attitude.

The traditional small-scale thinking is still prevalent among farmers. It instinctively resists the market and isolates them from the outside world. So the enclosed-type of production is strengthened, making it difficult for peasants to accept the norms of conduct of socialized large-scale production and adapt themselves to the changes in market supply and demand relations. Faced with the macrocontrol policy of the government, they ignore it completely. The conservativeness of small-peasant thinking and satisfaction with things as they are produce a form of laziness in the new situation. Moreover, efforts to remold this type of thinking are hampered by the stubborn fact of too many people and too little land. The conclusion we must come to is that agriculture will not escape from the situation of small-scale production for a fairly long time to come, and it will be difficult to realize agricultural intensification and scale management. The situation of low-level agricultural technology and productive forces will also still exist for a long time to come. The scattered household production is seriously divorced from market demand. It is difficult for many farmers to get correct market information, and so in production they often blindly follow others, resulting in unstable production.

In rural economic development, the positive and negative psychological factors in the farmers show that both new things and old things exist at the same time, and the farmers sometimes forge ahead and sometimes draw back.

(VII) Providing Assistance for Poor Areas and Promoting the Common Development of the Rural Areas

For the common development of rural areas it is urgent to provide assistance for poor areas in an efficient way. The problems which need to be solved are as follows:

1. Strengthening leadership and exercising macro control.

Strengthening the work of providing assistance for poor areas and developing the market economy are demands of modern socialist construction, the urgent desire of the people in poor mountain areas, and a glorious but arduous task. The Party and government leading organs at all levels should take close attention to this. The main leaders of the leading organs at all levels should make deep investigations of the realities of the lives of poor people. Capable cadres should be sent to work in the poorest areas and special organs for providing assistance for poor areas should be set up. It is a long-term and an arduous task to change the backwardness of these poor areas. The important instructions concerning the lightening of the burdens on the farmers formulated by the central government should be earnestly implemented. Inhabitants of the poor areas should have to turn over no more than five percent of their average annual per capita net income.

The efficient carrying out of practical macrocontrol is the prerequisite for guaranteeing the work of providing assistance to poor areas and promoting their opening up. It is also an important step to seize opportunities; by paying too much attention to stability we may miss chances for development. We also must not act blindly in spite of conditions and possibilities which encourage us to do so. We must keep in mind the real meaning of the market economy; it is not an anarchical free economy. Such tendencies are strictly controlled even in the capitalist world nowadays. As far as macro control is concerned, the market economies of the advanced countries all operate under strict standards, and we can learn from them.

CHPATER V CHANGING FUNCTIONS OF THE GOVERNMENT

Experience both at home and abroad in providing assistance for poor areas and helping them open up teaches us that the following macrocontrol aspects should be properly handled: First, funds and materials which have been earmarked for providing assistance to poor areas must be used rationally. The infrastructure and basic industries in poor mountain areas should be safeguarded as far as possible; the readjustment of the industrial structure should be promoted; the development of rural enterprises, and secondary and tertiary industry should be pushed ahead. Sources of all kinds of investment funds, including new loans, recovery reloaning, all kinds of stocks and bonds, and other forms of raising funds should be put under strict management and supervision. The management of the setting up of all kinds of open economic zones and real estate should be strengthened. Second, market management should be improved. Farmers who live in scattered communities in broad expanses of poor mountain areas lack transport facilities and live far from cities. As a result, they lack commodity awareness and have difficulty both in buying and selling things. The government departments concerned should actively develop the market to get the farmers used to operating in a market economy. Third, the state's macrocontrol function is important in the opening up of resources, such as forests, minerals and water resources in the poor mountain areas. These resources should be made use of in a planned and organized way; indiscriminate felling of trees should be strictly forbidden. Resources should be protected and used rationally. Fourth, the macrocontrol role of credit, taxes and law should be brought into full play.

2. Broadening the mind, changing the outlook and steadily providing assistance for poor areas and their opening up.

From now on, in the work of providing assistance for poor areas and their opening up we must adapt our thinking to the new situation of the market economy, broaden our minds and change outlooks. With the necessary support of the government and using the market as a guide, the advantages of all types of resources should be brought into full play along with the development of the commodity economy, mainly on the basis of self-reliance. The

217

concept of the planned economy should be replaced by the concept of the market economy. The following new concepts should be formed. Necessary funds are to be circulated in the market and managerial channels are to be opened wider. The concepts of monoculture and decentralized management will be abandoned. The concept of giving full play to comprehensive advantages, overall advantages and complementary advantages will be fostered. In the work of providing assistance to poor areas and their opening up, the administrative concept of management should be abandoned and the mechanism of market competition should be applied in opening up. The traditional methods of making use of personnel should be reformed. In making use of personnel, the habits of demanding perfection and promoting people according to status should be changed. We should boldly promote and make full use of young and middle-aged cadres who have both ability and integrity, and are bold in the pursuit of opening up. We should firmly support capable cadres who do well in reform and opening up, and in providing assistance for poor areas and their opening up.

The setting up of a market economic structure entails a process of gradual development and uninterrupted perfection. The work of shaking off poverty and becoming prosperous in poor mountain areas is a longer process of hard struggle. Both developing a market economy and changing the backwardness of poor mountain areas entail a process of proceeding in an orderly way and step by step. At present, these areas where people don't have adequate food and clothing have very poor natural conditions, low degree of social development, backward economy and culture, poor transport facilities and undeveloped commodity economy. Besides, some of these areas are subject to natural calamities, lack sufficient water for people and animals or are afflicted by endemic diseases. At the same time, though the problems of adequate food and clothing for people in some poor mountain areas have been solved, the situation is not very stable. When these areas meet natural calamities some of the local people still can not get enough food and clothing. Therefore, we should never neglect the work of providing assistance to the poor areas

CHPATER V CHANGING FUNCTIONS OF THE GOVERNMENT

and their opening up while we are setting up a socialist market economy structure.

3. The market economy will be developed gradually and preferential policies will be implemented continuously.

From a long-term point of view, developing a market economy is the way to rationally make use of the resources in poor mountain areas, promote commodity circulation, and improve culture and education, and hygiene. We should promote the development of the economy, quicken the work of shaking off poverty and becoming prosperous and create favorable conditions for economic advance in the poor areas. But the poor mountain areas suffer from bad conditions and their economic bases are weak. For a long time they depended heavily on government subsidies and, in consequence, the ability of the local people to help themselves is very low, as is their market awareness. Therefore, if we do not proceed from actual conditions, but copy indiscriminately the methods by which the market economy has been developed elsewhere, efforts to develop the economies of the poor mountain areas will come to naught. For example, if the state's subsidies for certain means of production, such as chemical fertilizer, diesel oil, and agricultural plastic sheeting were to be totally abolished and these things were to be sold at market prices, the peasants in poor mountain areas would not be able to afford them. Therefore, grain production would be hampered. Also, in the absence of macro control, the implementation of market prices for timber, minerals and energy resources would lead to severe deforestation, destruction of resources and damage to the environment. This is because farmers in poor mountain areas lack commodity awareness and awareness of business managerial methods, so their products fall short of market needs. They often can not sell their products, or they are cheated by middlemen.

To avoid these problems, the following policy measures should be adopted:

First, developing the market economy is a gradual process. We should carry out the development of the market economy according to the conditions of social economic development in different regions and taking measures suited to local conditions.

The methods of imposing uniformity in all cases and being overanxious for quick results should be avoided. The natural, economic and social conditions in poor mountain areas are not as good as in the plain regions, and far inferior to those in the developed coastal areas. Therefore, proceeding from actual conditions, we should adopt practical and effective measures and actively create the necessary conditions to guide the broad masses of the farmers to march on the right track for developing the market economy.

Second, special policies should be implemented continuously by the state for poor mountain areas. To guarantee the stable development of grain production there the state should continue to provide subsidies for the supply of chemical fertilizer, diesel oil, agricultural plastic sheeting and some other means of production, and provide low-interest and flexible loans to the farmers. In taxation too, the state should give appropriate preferential treatment to the farmers. Some special policies should continue to be implemented in counties where the yearly average net income per person is below 300 yuan and the farmers are not self-sufficient in grain. Such policies should embrace agricultural tax, regulation tax for investment of fixed assets, funds for the construction of key state projects in the fields of energy resources and communications. The deadlines for loans used for the construction of agricultural infrastructure and forestry should be extended; the turnover rate and rate of utilization of discount loans for supporting poor areas should not be changed within five years. The bad debt rate for providing assistance to poor areas should be raised. For local special products which are highly competitive on the world market, the poor mountain areas should be allowed to set up their own import and export corporations, which are independent in management and assume sole responsibility for their profits or losses. The departments for providing assistance for poor areas should be able to use some of their funds to help set up such businesses.

4. Strengthening the construction of agricultural infrastructure to create the conditions for developing the market economy.

The construction of infrastructure must be strengthened in

CHPATER V CHANGING FUNCTIONS OF THE GOVERNMENT

order to get rid of the backwardness of the poor mountain areas, and gradually improve the conditions of production and life there. The comprehensive opening up of agriculture should be carried out in conjunction with irrigation and water conservancy projects. The focus should be on creating farmland which can ensure stable yields despite drought or excessive rain. Industries which can open up and use the local resources, lead the farmers in shaking off poverty and becoming prosperous, and form important sources of revenue for the counties should be set up. Effective measures should be adopted to mobilize the masses to build small-sized water conservancy projects in order to solve the problem of supplying enough water for people and animals. Areas with favorable factors should actively develop small-sized hydropower stations, and make active use of sources of wind and solar energy.

5. Policies should encourage the exploitation of resources in poor mountain areas and stress should be placed on the development of backbone projects.

Since 1949 the state has done a lot of work for the opening up of the poor mountain areas, and a certain amount of success has been achieved. But it has not extended the same care to these areas as it has to the east coastal areas. It is now realized that the country's unexploited resources are mainly concentrated in these areas, and development there will contribute to the permanent, coordinated and stable development of the overall national economy. Therefore, according to the situation of natural resources in the poor mountain areas, both the central and local governments should adopt policies favorable to these areas in exploiting the resources. Stress should be placed on some backbone projects, which can open up and make use of the local resources and can bring along the regional economic development.

In recent years the state has put stress on comprehensive agricultural opening up in the poor mountain areas in China's central and western regions. For example, the state has arranged some agricultural comprehensive opening up projects in Guizhou Province, Gansu Province, Ningxia Hui Autonomous Region and Xinjiang Uygur Autonomous Region.

6. Horizontal connections should be strengthened and the policy of opening to the outside world fully implemented.

For changing resources advantages in poor mountain areas into commodity advantages and promoting the development of the market economy, horizontal economic connections must be strengthened and the policy of opening to the outside world vigorously implemented. We should make full use of the advantages of the poor areas, which have long border lines and have many border trade ports. In these favorable conditions, we can actively open up trade with neighboring countries, absorb foreign investment, and introduce technology, skills and managerial experience. By so doing we can absorb something by learning from others' strong points. At the same time, we should also actively export labor services and technology, and set up Sino-foreign joint enterprises and solely Chinese-owned enterprises. The exchanges between the eastern and western regions will be strengthened, as will relations between the urban and rural areas. Thus, the traditional isolation of the poor rural areas will be eroded. Preferential measures will be adopted to encourage people from other provinces, cities and regions to come to the poor mountain areas and set up experimental enterprises. The cadres in the poor mountain areas and cadres in the developed regions will be organized to study and learn from each other. Counterpart supporting groups will be organized between big and medium-sized cities, and developed regions. Exchange programs and counterpart supporting groups are organized between cadres from Shaanxi Province in the west and cadres from Jiangsu and Shandong provinces in the east. People from poor mountain areas in Zhejiang Province are arranged to set up new investment and development zones in developed regions and suburbs of cities. All these steps play an important role in promoting the development of the market economy and in getting rid of backwardness. Their experiences are worth learning from and promoting.

7. The development of rural enterprises should be speeded up.

It is only since 1979 that China's rural enterprises have sprung up all of a sudden. They have made great contributions to

CHPATER V CHANGING FUNCTIONS OF THE GOVERNMENT

rural development and the growth of the national economy. The rural enterprises have become a vigorous leading force in the market economy. But for many reasons the development speed of rural enterprises is quite different in different places. The development of the enterprises in the poor mountain areas of China's central and western regions is very slow, leading to an economic gaps between the eastern section and the central and western parts. The development of rural enterprises in poor mountain areas should take into account the needs of markets both at home and abroad, and be based their advantages in local resources. Except for what is forbidden by law, there are no restrictions on the development in poor mountain areas, so long as the products have good quality and good sales, and can improve the economic environment. The development of rural enterprises should proceed from the comprehensive conditions of local markets, resources, talent, transportation, and energy resources. Besides, the development measures should be suited to local conditions. The rural enterprises should be first of all relatively concentrated in small towns, and later expand their spheres of development.

8. Striving to do a good job of spreading knowledge and taking science and technology as the mainstay.

Having qualified personnel is the most important thing for the work of providing assistance to the poor areas and helping them open up. First of all, we should do a good job of spreading knowledge. From a long-term point of view, the development of basic education is a must for raising the quality of laborers in poor mountain areas. Education is a thing of vital and lasting importance. So, we should make plans to increase the investment in knowledge by developing and popularizing primary education first, and then vocational education, and speeding up the training of all kinds of qualified personnel. The leading departments at different levels should make up their minds to adopt effective measures to create an environment and mechanism to boldly introduce, train and make use of qualified personnel. We should encourage able cadres to engage in the work of providing assistance to the poor areas and helping them open up and develop the market economy. Graduates from universities and special secondary schools will be encouraged to work in poor mountain areas. People from scientific research institutions, universities, special secondary schools, academic societies and democratic parties are welcome to help us formulate and perfect the plans for the work for providing assistance to poor areas. They can give people guidance, take part in making decisions on economic technology, build up bases for technical experiments and demonstrations. The most-needed scientific and technological achievements should be introduced from other places for raising the level of the productive forces, and getting better economic results.

9. Developing the commodity economy and strengthening the structure of social services.

From the long-term point of view, by relying on a self-sufficient farming economy and not developing the commodity economy it will be impossible to solve the problem of food and clothing, shake off poverty and reach prosperity. To develop the commodity economy we must face the market, rely on local resources, optimize the industrial structure, reform traditional industry, open up new industries to provide more employment chances for people in poor mountain areas, tap new financial resources and increase incomes. Within a region, whatever industry is developed, we should take measures suited to the local conditions and give full play to local advantages.

We should organize individual households to develop the commodity economy and provide more and better services. In the past, in rural areas supply and marketing cooperatives, commercial and trade departments, goods and materials departments, and grain departments, all put stress on service after production. But what we need now are services before and after production. These departments should be allowed to form service-type economic entities gradually. At the same time, we should energetically support and encourage capable persons and specialized households in rural areas to set up all kinds of service-type organizations. With the deepening of the development of the reform of the economic structure we will gradually transmit certain functions of the government which directly organize production to service organizations and trade associations. By so doing, we will enable

CHPATER V CHANGING FUNCTIONS OF THE GOVERNMENT

these organizations to become a powerful force which can keep in contact with the numerous scattered households, and help the farmers develop the commodity economy.

10. Continuously mobilizing people from state organs and other circles to take part in activities for providing assistance to poor areas.

In recent years people from all circles, cadres from central organs and local Party and government organs, soldiers, policemen, people from mass organizations, democratic personages, people from industrial and commercial circles, people from scientific research institutions, and people from universities and special secondary schools have all taken part in the activities for providing assistance to poor areas. These people have done a lot of work to enable the Party and the government to maintain close links with the masses. These activities have promoted the opening up and construction in poor mountain areas and should be maintained for a long time to come. In particular, each department should keep in contact with a poor area to help it shake off poverty and become prosperous.

图书在版编目(CIP)数据

中国农村的经济改革与发展:英文/高尚全,迟福林主编.
—北京:外文出版社,1997
(中国市场经济研讨丛书)
ISBN 7-119-00697-5

Ⅰ.中… Ⅱ.①高… ②迟… Ⅲ.①农村经济-经济改革-中国-英文②农村经济-经济发展-中国-英文 Ⅳ.F320.2

中国版本图书馆CIP数据核字(96)第12869号

责任编辑　陈有昇
封面设计　唐　宇

中国农村的经济改革与发展

高尚全、迟福林主编

*

ⓒ外文出版社
外文出版社出版
(中国北京百万庄大街24号)
邮政编码100037
北京外文印刷厂印刷
中国国际图书贸易总公司发行
(中国北京车公庄西路35号)
北京邮政信箱第399号　邮政编码100044
1997年(大32开)第1版
(英)
ISBN 7-119-00697-5 /F·34(外)
02500
4-E-3096P